W9-BMW-534

Contents

Introduction:
Passing the Baton

The critical moment in any relay race comes when one runner passes the baton on to the next runner. Regardless of how well each may run individually, the race will be lost if they drop the baton. The runner receiving the baton must start soon enough so that time is not lost, but cannot outrun the one who is finishing the first leg of the race. For one important moment, both teammates have a firm grip on the baton. Then the tired, first runner releases, and the fresh sprinter accelerates toward the finish line.

The "generation gap" at times so evident in American culture is a sociological variation of the difficulties in passing the baton from the members of one generation to those of another. Families, businesses, institutions, and churches each have codes and rituals, some written but many unwritten, which guide them through this critical period. But what happens when there is confusion and two runners reach for the same baton? What happens when heirs vie for the same inheritance, when ambitious executives aspire to the senior executive's office, or when differing groups each claim the authority of ecclesiastical tradition? Who gets the house when a marriage ends in divorce? Constitutions, laws, charters, bylaws, and policies are framed to handle such conflicts and provide procedures by which they can be resolved without destroying the corporate body or social entity. Even within well established legal or social restraints the conflict can be vindictive. Persons can be hurt and institutions damaged.

The Johannine Epistles originated from a maelstrom of conflict. The baton was about to be dropped. The first generation of church leadership had "finished the race and kept the faith"; it had guided a small band of believers through the difficulties of breaking with the synagogue and the Jewish community. Under the leadership of the Beloved Disciple that group of Jewish Christians had lived by a new commandment: love one another even if it means laying down your life for a friend. The Beloved Disciple was their living link with the Lord they worshiped. He reminded them of what Jesus had said and done: his teachings and his signs (i.e., the things he did which pointed both to who he was and to a life they could barely glimpse). Especially prominent in the Beloved Disciple's teaching and preaching were Jesus' last night, his death on the cross, and his resurrection from the dead. This disciple guided them into new understandings. He bore a faithful witness and courageously confronted the world with the proclamation that Jesus was the Christ and the Son of God. Even against adversity the church grew, but the leadership of one generation can pass quickly.

Although some thought the Beloved Disciple would not die before the Lord came, time proved them wrong. Others now had to pick up the baton he had carried so well. There was little organization; they were a community of faith, a fellowship of believers. Leaders served as needed; formal offices and statements of doctrine and polity were still fixtures of the future. The believers were conscious of the Spirit, but certain prophets and teachers claimed the direction of the Spirit for teachings which others judged to be departures from the beliefs they had inherited from the earlier generation. These prophets and teachers apparently proclaimed that the revelation of God in Jesus was salvific; his death had no particular saving significance. In fact they may have suggested that the Spirit of God had left Jesus before he died. Could divinity suffer the corruption of death? There were also differences within the church over the place of sin in the life of a believer. What was sin, unbelief or unrighteousness? Could believers sin, or were believers freed from sin by virtue of their new birth as children of God? When conflict erupted in the community, various individuals charged others—and maybe each other—with violating the basic ethic of the community, unqualified love for one another. This ethic was established on Jesus' "new commandment": "that you love one another as I have loved you" (John 13:34).

When the conflict became more hostile one group severed relations with the other. Charges and accusations were made. Each group claimed it had the truth of the gospel and carried the baton passed on from the Beloved Disciple and the earlier generation of believers. Each group may also have appealed to the Gospel of John, the gospel left by the previous generation, for authority for its teachings. Neither the Beloved Disciple nor the Gospel of John is ever explicitly quoted or cited in the Johannine Epistles, but the first epistle in particular provides direction for how the "spiritual Gospel" is to be understood. Areas the Gospel leaves ambiguous are clarified. (For that reason, numerous cross references between the Epistles and the Gospel are included in the commentary. By consulting the related passages the reader will become sensitive to Johannine idioms, fresh nuances, and the context for understanding the Epistles.) Later generations of believers may even owe the preservation of the Gospel of John and its continued use by the church at large to the interpretations of it provided by the first epistle. Had alternative interpretations prevailed, the Gospel of John might have died with Gnosticism. Its first commentators were gnostics, and it seems to have been especially popular among gnostic groups during the second century. That its Christology was finally embraced by the "orthodox" church is due in no small part to the anonymous writer of the Johannine Epistles.

Although the standard detective questions of NT scholarship—Who wrote it? When? and Where?—are not crucial to the task of interpreting these letters for preaching; basic assumptions operative in this commentary can be indicated briefly without pausing to attempt to justify them. The three epistles were probably written about A.D. 100 by the same person, an elder (2 John 1; 3 John 1) of the church which had produced the Gospel of John. This church community was at the hub of a network of related house churches. Some of these may have been in the same city, perhaps Ephesus; others were located in nearby towns.

1 John was written to defend the church against attacks from and defections to a group that had separated itself from them. In form it is not a true letter, since it neither begins

nor ends like an epistle. It is also anonymous. Even in a situation where writings from the other group may have been circulating, the author does not identify himself by name or title. It is more a manifesto than an epistle; i.e., "a public declaration of intentions, motives, or views" (*Webster's Ninth New Collegiate Dictionary*). 1 John begins with an echo of the prologue of the Fourth Gospel, declares the understandings of the author's group on questions such as sin among believers, the incarnation, the love command, the role of the Spirit, and eschatological expectations. At each point, at least by implication, it distinguishes the group's beliefs from those of its rivals and rejects the latter as not just mistaken but satanic, inspired by the antichrist.

2 John is a short letter to a church closely related to the elder and the "mother church." In its content this letter resembles 1 John, repeating some of the same concerns without elaboration. Vocabulary, style, and content all suggest that the two epistles were written at about the same time and by the same person. The author was concerned that those who had crippled the "mother church" might also pose a danger to this "sister church." The church should not even greet those who did not share their confession. This short note provides a provisional affirmation and warning, promising that the elder hoped to visit them soon.

3 John is not concerned with the doctrinal threats alluded to in the other two letters. Instead, it is a personal letter addressed to Gaius concerning the problems caused by Diotrephes, who refused to show hospitality to those sent by the elder. This short letter offers tantalizing insights into the problems and developing organization of the early church. Diotrephes resisted the elder and asserted his leadership instead. Perhaps in an effort to prevent dissension and false teachings from reaching his church, Diotrephes had refused to receive those who came from the elder, and even excluded from the church those who did offer them hospitality. Consequently, the elder praised Gaius for his hospitality to "the brothers," criticized Diotrephes for his defiance, and added a note of commendation for one of the faithful, Demetrius. Unfortunately, persons mentioned in the letter are otherwise unknown.

Lines of authority were not yet clearly drawn in the early

church. The elder apparently exercised leadership by virtue of his association with the Beloved Disciple and the other tradition bearers of Johannine Christianity. All Johannine Christians, however, shared the anointing of the Holy Spirit; they were a community of "brothers" (3 John 3, 5, 10) and "friends" (3 John 15). Consequently, the elder could not simply assert the authority of his office; he could only appeal to the goodwill of a "beloved" brother.

Succeeding generations of Christians would have a longer heritage by which to judge beliefs, conduct, and leadership within the Christian community. These brief epistles cast a long shadow, however, for they provide a context for understanding the Gospel of John and its peculiar views of the incarnation and death of Christ, the Holy Spirit, life in the Christian community, and the hope for the future. They also reflect some of the struggles of the emerging church and set in relief the dangerous consequences of doctrines and organizational patterns it rejected. Study of these epistles brings the Johannine church and its writings to life and helps us appreciate nuances in the Fourth Gospel. More importantly, these epistles open for us profound insights into God's love, the practical consequences of false teachings, and the ideal of perfection in the life of a Christian. Invariably, they also cause us to reflect on whether we have been faithful to the heritage we have received from those who have gone before us and how we will pass the legacy of faith on to the next generation.

Specific suggestions regarding preaching themes are scattered throughout the exposition. Many of the chapter and section titles may serve as sermon starters, and other suggestions may be found in the introduction or conclusion of each chapter.

1 JOHN

The Word of Life
(1 John 1:1–4)

Good beginnings are always important, whether they are the beginning of a sermon, a book, a marriage, or a friendship. As a beginning for 1 John, the author gathered up many of the themes to be developed and presented these in a form reminiscent of the prologue of the Gospel of John. Just as we can be awkward when trying too hard to make a good first impression, the author left his piece with a clumsy opening by trying to pack too much into it. The first sentence runs through at least the middle of the third verse, and the result is what commentators have described as "bordering on incoherence" (Houlden), "the most complicated Greek in the Johannine corpus. . . . a grammatical obstacle course" (Brown), or "an incoherent sentence structure" (Grayston). Nevertheless, if the reader will pause to reflect on the phrases of this opening, they yield a distinctive mixture of profound affirmations. The sentence is composed of five relative clauses:

> What was from the beginning,
> what we have heard,
> what we have seen with our eyes,
> what we have beheld and our hands handled . . .
> what we have seen and heard. . . .

These clauses are interrupted by an intrusion (vs. 2), which restates the meaning of the phrase "concerning the word of life," and are followed by the main clause, we declare also to you,

and a purpose clause,

in order that you may have fellowship with us.

The remainder of the prologue to 1 John consists of a statement affirming that our fellowship is with the Father and his Son Jesus Christ, and a further statement of the purpose for writing this "epistle."

1 John begins with a statement of "what we have handled, seen, and heard." It calls for reflection on what we have touched, seen, or heard that has changed the nature of life for us. Common to many believers is a yearning for "A Faith to Hold On To." A sermon on this subject would emphasize that in Jesus God became tangible, visible, and audible; but it would also point out (see John 20:17) that faith and "the word of life" now remain as tangible, visible, and audible witnesses to Jesus.

From the Beginning

Deliberate echoes of both Genesis and the new genesis described in the prologue to the Gospel of John reverberate in the opening words of 1 John. The message of the epistle can be traced to what was "from the beginning." The meaning of this phrase is not defined here. Later *beginning* will be used in reference to the earliest days of the Johannine church and the proclamation of the gospel ("what you heard from the beginning"; see 2:7, 24; 3:11; 2 John 5–6). This proclamation was rooted in the ministry of Jesus, who is described in the Gospel as the *logos* which was with God from the beginning (John 1:1–2). The use of the neuter relative pronoun ("that which was") suggests that the author is thinking of the message of life rather than of Jesus himself, and is therefore recalling the earliest preaching of the church, which was rooted in Jesus. Because of its earlier uses in both John and Genesis, however, the word *beginning* echoes in Christian ears evoking earlier and earlier foundations of the Christian gospel.

The phrases that follow shift from what was to what "we" have experienced. Implicit here is the good news that ours is not a silent god, not an invisible god, not an immaterial god, yet no idol either (see 5:21). God has spoken to his people. They have heard him in the words of Jesus and seen him in the face of Jesus. Their hands have touched him. The elder emphasizes the <u>sensory perception of revelation</u>: "heard" (vss. 1, 3), "seen" (vss. 1, 2, 3), "beheld" (vs. 1), "handled" (vs. 1). In part, at least, the eschatological hope of a beatific vision, of seeing God, has already been realized (see 3:2). If the Johannine church was bedeviled by proponents of a doctrine which denied the incarnation, the elder's opening salvo ties the gospel, "the word of life," to what was seen and heard and handled. For him the incarnation is not dispensable. Apart from that life, there is no Life.

The "we" of the prologue links the faith of the community to the experience of its founders, especially, we may assume, the Beloved Disciple. *We* is used in a similar manner in the Gospel of John: in the prologue it affirms the glory of God beheld in the incarnation (John 1:14). Later in the Gospel the pronoun is used to comment on the role of the community (John 3:11). Jesus spoke of what he had seen and heard from the Father (John 3:32; 5:19; 8:28, 40; 15:15). The Beloved Disciple bore witness to what he had seen and heard (John 19:35; 21:24). The "we" who had gathered around him and helped him shape the tradition into the Gospel passed on what had been seen and heard "from the beginning," and now the elder was defending the community against the threat of division and false doctrine by appealing to the beliefs which had given the community its identity. By claiming the tradition of the Gospel, they (and we) may all participate in the revelation which was received by sensory experience. In time of threat it is not a bad strategy to return to the essentials, the core, the foundation on which all else depends. Just as families have "roots," so does the Christian community, and its taproot reaches deep into the mystery of the incarnation.

The Word of Life

At the heart of the gospel is a word about life. All of vs. 2 is an intrusion or parenthesis which interrupts the flow from vs. 1 to vs. 3. The phrase "concerning the word of life" means first the message of the gospel. The parenthesis relates the essence and quality of life promised by the gospel to the quality of life which was witnessed in Jesus of Nazareth. The

nature of eternal life as it is lived out in oneness and fellowship with the Father was revealed in Jesus' life. In trying to
make this point, confusion is introduced between the message which was heard and the person who was seen and handled. The focus here is not on the *logos* in the personalized
sense which it has in the prologue of the Gospel of John but
on the *life* Jesus gave and which has become the central fea-
ture of the gospel message. In Johannine thought eternal life
is that quality of life which belongs to God's children. It is
received by believing "in his name" (John 1:12); marked by a
new birth (John 3:3); sustained by participation in a new
family (John 20:17), flock (John 10), or vine (John 15); nour-
ished by living water and bread from heaven; and characterized by missionary and pastoral activities which require
bearing a faithful witness. Like Lazarus, those who share in
this life from another aeon will find that death is not the last
enemy but a passage—like sleep—a passage from life to life.
The heart of John's Gospel is that this life finds its beginning
and its end exclusively in the character of God as Father.
Moreover, this life has been revealed in Jesus, who makes it
available to all who receive him in faith.

We Declare to You

Because it is the nature of that life to draw others to it, the
two verbs for reception in vs. 2 (*manifested* and *seen*) are balanced by two verbs for transmission (*witness* and *declare*).
Paradoxically, this revelation is always for us, but never for
us alone. The gospel does not allow one to exclude either oneself or any other person from the life it offers, for to do so is
to fail to grasp its significance. Bearing witness, therefore, is
the principal duty of discipleship for Johannine Christians.
That witness may require denying inappropriate claims for
oneself (as John the Baptist did; John 1:19), sharing the ex-
citement of the gospel with one's neighbors (as the Samari-
tan woman did; John 4), declaring what we have experienced
(as the Beloved Disciple did; John 21:24), washing dirty feet
(as disciples are required to do; John 13), and even laying
down one's life (as a good shepherd does; John 10:11;
21:15–19). Both the writing and the preaching of 1 John,
therefore, are in a sense further fulfillments of the demand
that the revelation of eternal life makes on those who receive
it.

A Partial Fellowship

The last clause of this extended first sentence contains the first statement of the purpose for the writing of 1 John: "in order that you may have fellowship with us." What is at stake is not merely friendship or congenial relations. In Johannine dualism there are no gray areas. One is identified with either truth or falsehood, light or darkness. To have fellowship with the believing community (i.e., to have a part in it, to be in partnership with it) requires that one be an integral part of it. If one does not have fellowship with the community, then one is a part of the unbelieving world. On the other hand, 1 John is not a missionary tract for unbelievers but a communication with those who belong to the church but are in danger of turning from it. 1 John, therefore, is an appeal to those on the way to apostasy. For some it may have been the literary equivalent of the choice morsel Jesus offered to Judas before he went out into the night; it is "love's last appeal." The danger is that those who were still a part of the community might adopt beliefs and life-styles which the elder viewed as so deviant that further participation in the community of belief would be impossible. Some had already crossed that line (see 2:19).

For the elder the response of the readers is not merely a question of whether they will be a part of the community. The fellowship of his community is "with the Father and with his Son Jesus Christ." The implication is that apart from fellowship with the earthly community of faith there is no fellowship with God. The pluralism of the church today makes it difficult for us to grasp the exclusiveness of the spirit of 1 John, and when seen, that exclusiveness is offensive. Is one's access to God's fellowship controlled by adherence to orthodoxy in matters of faith or orthopraxy in relation to the mores of the church? What are the proper limits of toleration and diversity? Was the elder drawing the line too narrowly? Answers to the historical questions are hidden in the mists of antiquity, through which we can catch only occasional glimpses of the situation in which this writing came into being. The questions it poses, however, continue to be relevant for the church as it struggles for a more inclusive fellowship within the body of believers and as it attempts to formulate responses to secularism and religious pluralism. There can be no fellowship with that which is opposed to Christ's redemptive work. On the other hand, there can be no truly Christian fellowship which is not as inclusive as God's love. Until truth can be known more fully, life lived more purely, and the boundaries of our fellowship extended more widely, that fellowship will necessarily remain only a partial one. And—as 1 John reminds us—our fellowship is with the Father and his Son Jesus Christ.

An Incomplete Joy

Where fellowship is only partial, joy can never be complete. The elder had a genuine pastoral concern for those who were in danger of excluding themselves from fellowship with the Lord and his people, and from the eternal life which he offers. The individual triumphalism of those who celebrate their own salvation in the face of the damnation of others is certainly contrary to the spirit of Christianity. Can we sing "Oh that will be glory for me, glory for me, glory for me" when others are being destroyed by international, interracial, and interclass conflicts, when others are hungry or deranged by substance abuse, or victimized by those driven to crime? Partial joy is the perpetual condition of the Christian. Jesus left his joy to his followers (John 15:11; 16:20–24; 17:13), but that joy can never be complete so long as his redemptive work is still unfinished.

A sermon entitled "Partial Fellowship, Incomplete Joy" could help some Christians to move away from a self-centered piety to a more inclusive understanding of the nature of the church and God's redemptive work. We all know what it is like to live with partiality and incompleteness. This human condition may be heard as a call to become partners in a community of faith rather than as a rebuke for deficiencies in our personal piety.

The prologue to 1 John, therefore, reaches from "the beginning" through the present ("we declare") to the consummation of God's purposes, when partnership and joy can both be complete. That fulfillment, the elder declares, can come about only through the "word of life," and its realization will mean eternal life, i.e., that life which is the gift of God to all whose life and fellowship are with him and his Son, Jesus Christ.

The Dangers of Denying Sin
(1 John 1:5—2:2)

Following the opening paragraph, which sets a context for the rest of the epistle, the author turns directly to the problem: some Christians were denying that they were guilty of sin. In making this claim, they apparently thought that through their belief in Jesus as the one who revealed the Father they had become enlightened, free of sin. Indeed, if sin was regarded primarily as unbelief—as the Gospel of John seems to imply (16:8)—then they were no longer guilty of sin because they had accepted Jesus as the Christ, the Son of God. Strange as this logic may seem today, it prompted the elder to write a warning about the dangers of denying the reality of sin in one's life. Although the problem is rooted in the peculiar beliefs of the Johannine community regarding sin and salvation, the elder's warning continues to have value in a time when the denial of sin takes appealing new forms.

Verse 5 begins the first major section of the epistle. The phrase "this is the message" reappears in 3:11 and is taken by Raymond Brown as a key to the structure of the epistle. The message is disarmingly simple: *God is light*. The inference drawn from this assertion is that since there is no darkness in God, there can be no darkness in his followers. But this state of sinlessness does not follow automatically from believing in Jesus. 1 John 1:5—2:2 is organized around a series of conditional sentences. In all, there are six in this section. Each of these conditional sentences concerns the place of sin in the life of a Christian. Three express conditions which are viewed as misguided and destructive (1:6, 8, 10). The other three (1:7, 9; 2:1b–2) offer constructive alternatives. The three statements regarding the consequences of denying the reality of sin can serve as an outline for this section, with vs. 5 standing as an introduction and 2:1–2 functioning as a conclusion.

Since the three disapproved conditions each begin with the phrase "if we say . . . ," it is reasonable to assume that some

in the elder's community were actually making these asser-
tions. These conditional sentences do not represent hypothet-
ical situations or remote possibilities, but represent serious
claims of influential members of the community. The rest of
the community was in danger of accepting these views. Because the elder sees the implications of such teachings, he
writes 1 John to appeal to those who will still listen and to
urge them not to accept teachings which he regards as a departure from what they had received in the tradition of the
Johannine community. That tradition originated with the
Father and was given to the Son, who revealed these things
to "his own"; the Beloved Disciple bore witness to them; the
Johannine school which gathered around him functioned as
the bearer of the community's authoritative tradition; and
the elder wrote as a representative of that body to combat a
destructive innovation in the life of Johannine Christianity.

Further analysis of the three rejected conditions shows
that they have a similar form and develop progressively in
their seriousness:

> 1:6 a   If we say that we have fellowship with him
>   b   and continue to walk in darkness,
>   c   we are lying
>   d   and not doing the truth.
>
> 1:8 a   If we say that we have no sin,
>   b
>   c   we are deceiving ourselves
>   d   and the truth is not in us.
>
> 1:10 a   If we say that we have never sinned,
>   b
>   c   we are making him a liar
>   d   and his word is not in us.

Each of these verses begins with an "if" clause, but only in
vs. 6 does the "if" clause have a second part (vs. 6b). The
problem in vs. 6 is not a false claim; the author has already
said that their fellowship is with God (1:3). The problem is
hypocrisy. Some claim to have this fellowship but continue
to live in darkness. The conditions named in vss. 8 and 10
deal explicitly with the denial of sin, and again there may be
a progression. Interpreted as translated above, vs. 8 cites the
claim of those who say they are not now guilty of any sin.
Verse 10 advances to the claim of those who say they have

not sinned at all; i.e., they have never sinned. More obvious is
the progressive severity of the consequences of this path of
denial. Those who are guilty of hypocrisy or self-delusion,
claiming to have fellowship while walking in darkness, are
lying and not doing the truth (vs. 6cd). Those who say they
are not guilty of sin are deceiving themselves, and the truth
is not in them. Worst of all is the claim that one has never
sinned, for then one makes God a liar and his word cannot
abide in such persons.

Verses 1:7, 9, and 2:1–2 present a similar pattern. The repetition of the "if" clauses serves as a contrast to the claims of
the misguided opponents, while the variations in the "then"
or consequence clauses spell out the theological response of
the elder.

1:7 a *But* if we walk in the light as he is in the light,
    b we have fellowship with one another
    c and the blood of Jesus, his son, cleanses us from
      all sin.

1:9 a If we confess our sins,
    b he is faithful and just
    c so that he forgives the sins for us and cleanses us
      from all wrong.

2:1b–2 a If anyone does sin,
    b we have an advocate before the Father, Jesus
      Christ, the righteous one;
    c and he is a covering for our sins,
      and not for ours only but also for the whole
      world.

The "then" clauses offer a clear progression developing the
author's understanding of the saving significance of Jesus'
death, a matter the opponents apparently neglected in favor
of the confession of Jesus as a heavenly revealer. The "if"
clauses of these sentences are not as parallel as those of vss.
6, 8, and 10, but this may in part be due to a desire to answer
the claim of each of the rejected conditions:

1:6 a If we say that we have fellowship with him
    b and continue to walk in darkness, . . .
1:7 a *But* if we walk in the light as he is in the light, . . .
1:8 a If we say that we have no sin, . . .
1:9 a If we confess our sins, . . .
1:10 a If we say that we have never sinned, . . .
2:1b–2 a If anyone does sin, . . .

The logic of this progression is clear and simple. We cannot live in God's fellowship if our lives are darkened by sin. Moreover, we cannot deny the reality of sin, even in the life of a Christian; but if we confess our sin, God is sure to forgive us because his grace is assured by his righteousness. He has provided a means of forgiveness through the sacrificial death of Jesus.

The three sets of clauses outlined above, with their negative and then positive emphases, can easily serve as the framework for a timely sermon on the title of this chapter, "The Dangers of Denying Sin."

The Message We Have Heard: God Is Light (1:5)

Whereas Christology dominates the Gospel of John, 1 John is theocentric: it explores the nature of God's character. A short series of sermons could therefore appropriately be developed around the themes "God is light" (1:5), "God is just" (2:29), "God is love" (4:8, 16). The first affirmation, that God is light, is at home generally in the religious practices of the period and specifically in the tradition of the Johannine community. Light is universally regarded as a quality of the divine character, and it appears frequently in the OT, the Dead Sea Scrolls, Philo, and the gnostic and Mandean writings. The Gospel of John uses the image repeatedly: in the *logos* there was a life which was "the light of men" (John 1:4). This light shone in the world to enlighten all people (John 1:5, 9). Exposing as well as illuminating, the light brought judgment as well as salvation (John 3:19–21). Jesus himself was the light (John 8:12), and opened the eyes of those born into darkness (John 9). One who follows Jesus will never walk in darkness (John 8:12). Indeed, those who believe in him "may not remain in darkness" (John 12:46, RSV) but become "sons of light" (John 12:36).

The message stated in 1 John 1:5, therefore, would have been readily accepted by all members of the Johannine community. Its nuance in this context is that since there is no darkness in God there can be no darkness (i.e., no sin) in the children of God. The elder's opponents would have agreed, but they apparently thought that merely by virtue of belief Christians had a new nature and could not be guilty of sin. Here they parted ways with the elder. Much as he may have wanted to affirm the ideal of Christian perfection, the elder recognized the reality of sin in the lives of believers and saw another, more difficult, road to perfection.

The Consequences of Hypocrisy: Deceit (1:6–7)

Verse 6 pinpoints the problem of contradiction between the claims one may make and one's way of life. The Johannine Christians claimed fellowship with God. No higher claim can be made for one's life, for it implies that one has come to know the character of God and been drawn into a continuing relationship with God. In fact it should mean that the character of God has become the transforming reality for one's life: all of life is lived in response to God's grace.

Some who made that claim, however, gave no evidence of "light" in their lives. *To walk* was a common idiom meaning "to live" (compare Mark 7:5; Acts 21:21; Rom 6:4; Gal 5:16; Eph 4:1; and in the Johannine Epistles: 1 John 2:6, 11; 2 John 4, 6; 3 John 3, 4). The Gospel of John associates darkness with evil deeds (3:19), so "walking in darkness" would communicate that one's life gave no evidence of the transformation claimed by those who said they had fellowship with God.

For the elder more was involved. Already he had said that the Johannine community had fellowship with God (1:3). It was unthinkable that one could have fellowship with God and be alienated from the community of the "children of God" (a term of central significance in the community's gospel). Fellowship with God requires that one participate in the community of those who find their life in him.

Those who hypocritically claim fellowship with God are liars and are not "doing" (i.e., acting in or living by) the truth. These are not mild terms. Coming from the elder, they identify the condemned as deceivers whose father is not God but the devil (John 8:44), false prophets who speak under the influence of the Spirit of Deception (2:22; 4:1, 6). If *truth* is that which conforms to reality, especially the ultimate reality of God's character and grace, then those who are not living in truth have no integrity. They are not integers, not whole numbers. Their lives deny their claims and confirm that they are deceivers who may be deceived themselves.

On the other hand, if one walks in the light, that person has fellowship not only with God but with others also (vs. 7ab).

Living under the reality of God's grace makes community possible. It makes it possible for us to have the kind of relationship with one another which God seeks to have with us. The elder is already thinking of the "new commandment," that we love one another as he has loved us (John 13:34; 1 John 2:7–11; 4:7).

The latter part of vs. 7 comes as a surprise. Sin has not been mentioned explicitly in the preceding verses. The reference to the blood of Jesus seems intrusive, and the language of cleansing from sin is more appropriate for an explanation of how one becomes a Christian. Here, however, the elder is dealing with the problem of sin in the life of a believer. The significance of Jesus' death is somewhat ambiguous in the Gospel of John both because John places so much emphasis on the significance of the incarnation and Jesus' role as revealer and because his death is portrayed not as a sacrifice but as an enthronement and exaltation to the Father. Some Johannine Christians may well have believed that they were saved by receiving the knowledge of God revealed by Jesus rather than by his death. Moreover, if the opponents denied that Jesus really came in flesh (4:2), they may also have denied that the *logos* could have died. If there is any substance to these inferences, the elder may be reclaiming a neglected part of the earlier tradition, drawing the community closer to a view of the death of Jesus such as we find elsewhere in early Christianity (e.g., Rom 5:10; Phil 2:8; Col 1:22). Whereas the Fourth Gospel spoke of being cleansed by his word (John 15:3), 1 John changes to the cultic language of being cleansed by blood (see Lev 17:11; Col 1:20; Heb 9:22; 1 Peter 1:19; Rev 1:5; 7:14). The implication in this context, therefore, would be that we are saved not just by Jesus' revelation but by his death. Believers, moreover, can continue to find cleansing from sin through the same means by which they first came to the light of God's grace. Such views would have been sharply debated by the elder's opponents.

The Consequences of Denying Sin: Self-delusion (1:8–9)

The words "If we say that we have no sin" may well echo the claim of those who would protest any further need for cleansing. "To have sin" is a Johannine idiom meaning to be

guilty of sin (see John 9:41; 15:22, 24; 19:11). We do not know
the precise basis for their claim. They may have thought that
in Christ they were new creations (2 Cor 5:17), immune from
the dangers of sin. They may have thought that since they
had the Spirit (3:24; 4:13) they were delivered from sin, that
they had attained such perfection that sin was no longer a
threat, or that sin meant only unbelief (John 16:8). Whatever
the origin of their view, it gave them a false confidence. The
elder therefore points out the further consequences of denying sin. Such a denial can only mean that we have so fallen
under the power of the Spirit of Deception (4:6; 3:7) that we
ourselves are its victims; we have deceived ourselves.

The consequence of being deceived is that the truth is not
in us. The thought here, as throughout the Epistles, is dualistic. One resides in either truth or falsehood, light or darkness, good or evil, life or death, Christ or the antichrist. If the
truth is not in us, therefore, there is no possibility that we
can live in fellowship with God. Such dualism may seem
overly rigid to contemporary ears, but it sharpens the seriousness of sin in the life of a Christian. Denying the presence
of sin excludes any possibility for dealing with it effectively.
One who denies the presence of sin cannot have the cleansing
of confession, the freedom born of forgiveness, or the tri-
umph which can come from conscientious effort to change
one's pattern of life.

Confession is the avenue to the power of the other sphere of
life. 1 John here puts the kind of premium on confession of
sin that the Johannine writings usually put on confessing
Jesus as the Christ (John 1:20; 9:22; 12:42; 1 John 2:23; 4:2, 3,
15; 2 John 7). Confession may begin with acknowledging our
own sinfulness, but true confession is motivated by remorse
and repentance, trusts that God is willing to forgive and
cleanse, is fulfilled in worship and the praise of God's goodness, and carries us toward the goal of pure lives lived under
God's grace. The alternation between the singular and the
plural (*sin* or *sins*) carries little difference in meaning. If anything, the plural allows the inference that not just unbelief
but all unrighteous deeds are sin.

The "then" clause of vs. 9 amplifies the latter part of vs. 7.
"Cleansing" is still emphasized, but the expansion grounds
the possibility of forgiveness in the character of God: "he is

faithful and just" (see Micah 7:18–20). Jesus shared in the character of God (2:1); he did not do something God was unwilling to do. These qualities must also characterize the "children of God" (2:29; 3:7). The result, and evidence, of God's faithfulness and justice is that he forgives us and cleanses us. Forgiveness means that we are released from our sin; it no longer holds us captive. This cultic language for cleansing from wrongdoing finds new meaning today in psychological release. If some wrongdoing leaves us feeling dirty, the assurance of forgiveness frees us from that dirt and allows us to feel clean again.

The Consequences of Claiming Perfection: Blasphemy (1:10)

The community was composed of those who had come to believe in Jesus as the Christ, the Son of God, and who had been forgiven and cleansed of sin. They lived with the ideal of a sinless life, and some apparently took the further step of denying that they sinned, or that they had sinned, or possibly that they had ever sinned. The problem of sin after one had become a Christian was particularly acute for the Johannine community. Even if confession were necessary, did this apply to believers or only to those who had not yet been cleansed from sin? How can believers also be sinners? They may have reasoned that if they were God's children, and he was righteous and sinless, then they must be equally sinless. The claim implied here is the third in the series that began in vss. 6 and 8. If there is a progression in the series, then this claim may deny that they had ever sinned, or that they had sinned after they became Christians.

The ultimate consequence of denying sin in one's life is not just self-deception but blasphemy: we make God a liar. There was ample evidence in Scripture for the claim that all had sinned (Prov 20:9; 1 Kings 8:46). To deny sin was therefore to deny the truth of God's word. Someone had to be lying; either God or those who claim they have no sin. Yet it is the devil who is the Father of Lies (John 8:44), so those who deny sin must be under his power rather than God's. Moreover, those who reject the truth of God's word cannot have it abiding within them. That word goes forth from the mouth of God to accomplish his will (Isa 55:11; see Col 3:16; James

1:21), but it finds no home in those who cannot see their own sinfulness and therefore cut themselves off from God's redemptive work.

Jesus Christ: A Righteous Advocate (2:1–2)

The first sentence of the second chapter gives a second statement of the elder's reason for writing. In 1:4 he had said that he was writing so that their joy might be fulfilled; here he says he is writing so that they might not sin. This second statement grows directly out of the preceding verses. The elder shares the desire and the ideal of those who hold that belief and sin are irreconcilable and that believers cannot sin. Opponents should not construe what he has written to mean that he is condoning sin. He is not arguing that they may sin because they can be forgiven; he is arguing that they cannot deny that they sin, even though they are believers. The elder writes to them as "my children," a term that is used often for the Johannine church (2:1, 12, 28; 3:7, 18; 4:4, 5:21), and is apparently drawn from John 13:33 and such OT references as Isa 8:16, 18; 54:13; and Deut 11:19.

On the other hand, if they do sin, they have an advocate or an intercessor (Greek, *parakletos*) before the Father. In the NT this term is peculiar to the Johannine writings. *Parakletos* is difficult to translate but seems to be drawn from legal parlance. In the Gospel of John, Jesus says that the Holy Spirit will be a Paraclete for the disciples. He will teach them all things (14:26) and convict the world of sin (16:8). There are distinct parallels between the roles of the three leading interpreters in the Johannine tradition: Jesus, who interprets the Father; the Holy Spirit, who will interpret Jesus; and the Beloved Disciple, who interprets Jesus for the Johannine community. In the Beloved Disciple, no doubt, the community saw the Paraclete at work. Why then do the Johannine Epistles never mention the Beloved Disciple, never use the term "Holy Spirit," and never call the Spirit the "Paraclete"? Several answers are possible. The most pertinent is probably that the Beloved Disciple had ceased to be a significant figure for the elder's opponents. The opponents claimed direct authority as prophets and teachers endowed with the Spirit. To counter this claim, the elder asserts that Jesus is the *parakletos*, thereby shifting the emphasis from the authority conveyed by the Spirit to the authority of Jesus as conveyed by the tradition of the community. The opponents could not reject the claim that Jesus was the Paraclete because it was supported by the Gospel of John (14:16, "another Paraclete"). The elder's point was that because the "children" were within the Johannine community they had fellowship with Jesus, the Paraclete. Those who claimed the Spirit had no greater authority. Moreover, precisely as Paraclete (advocate or intercessor), Jesus made intercession for the sins of the church.

Like the book of Hebrews (4:14–16), 1 John emphasizes Jesus' sinlessness (3:5, 7) in connection with his role in mediating forgiveness. Jesus is the righteous one, who is uniquely capable of forgiving sin. The Greek word *hilasmos* occurs only here and in 4:10 in the NT, but a cognate term appears in Rom 3:25 and Heb 9:5, and the verbal form occurs in Luke 18:13 and Heb 2:17. The term is drawn from the cultic act of offering a sacrifice to remove the offense of sin, which separates the worshiper from God. Hence it may be translated "propitiation," "expiation," or "atonement." The primary emphasis in this context is not the anger of God but the role of Jesus in covering or removing the sin and cleansing the sinner. Through his own initiative in sending Jesus to reveal and remove sin, God provided the means by which sin can be forgiven, even the sin of believers. As C. H. Dodd commented, linking this verse with 1:9, "Our forgiveness rests upon the justice and faithfulness of God, not upon the possibility of averting His anger" (*The Johannine Epistles*, p. 26).

The last clause of this section turns from preoccupation with the immediate problem to the universal and evangelistic force of the message that God is light (1:5). What God has done for the Johannine church he has done for all. The mission of Jesus was not just for us but for the whole world. We may become so preoccupied with theological questions or so obsessed with our own sin that we neglect the missionary demands of our faith. The final clause may be the most significant countermeasure of all. Preoccupation with our own perfection may become sin itself. The only effective remedy then is to become concerned about mediating the forgiveness effected by Jesus' death to those who are all too aware of the destructive power of sin. If Jesus did not make atonement for the whole world, could we believe that he has forgiven us?

This section of 1 John offers us a penetrating exhibition of the dangers of denying the presence of sin in our lives. That denial, of course, can take a variety of forms, all dangerous. How do we deny sin today? By refusing to take God seriously? By assuming that how we live does not matter? By refusing to see how we are compromised and corrupted by impure motives and desires while exposing the dirty laundry of others? The splinter and the beam syndrome can be practiced by individuals or nations, ethnic groups or religious denominations. Perhaps one factor in the contemporary neglect of sin is that we do not seriously believe that any other style of life is possible. We do not actually believe that the Word of Life can enable us to enjoy an entirely different quality of life as children who share the fellowship of a faithful and just God.

A sermon or series of sermons on dealing with hypocrisy, self-deception, and the subtle ways in which we deny sin could provide an opportunity for a church to recommit itself to honesty, spiritual health and fitness, and devotion to Jesus Christ.

The Command to Love
(1 John 2:3–11)

Even more basic than recognizing the reality of sin in one's life is the question of whether we know God or not. Having dealt with the dangers of denying sin, the elder turns to the hypocrisy of claiming to know God when one's life gives no evidence of such knowledge.

Those who claimed to be sinless could quite naturally also claim to have an intimate knowledge of God, which they probably also viewed as conveying salvation. Such at least was the common assumption of Hellenistic thought, the mystery cults, and the later gnostic groups. The claim to possess knowledge of God was an important ingredient in ancient religions. Plato maintained that men were enlightened and delivered from the material world by knowledge of the real world. His thought influenced later religious views, and its effect can be seen in the Alexandrian Jewish interpreter Philo: "The supreme end . . . is knowledge of Him who truly is, who is the first and most perfect Good, from whom as from a fountain all partial goods are poured upon the world and those in it" (*The Decalogue* 81). The Gospel of John also describes the goal of religious experience as the knowledge of God: "And this is eternal life, that they know thee the only true God, and Jesus Christ whom thou hast sent" (John 17:3, RSV). Clearly, the elder's opponents claimed a saving knowledge of God along with freedom from sin, but how could such a claim be confirmed or discredited? What tests could one apply to verify or deny such knowledge of God? To these the elder now directed the attention of his readers.

Jeremiah looked forward to a new covenant which he described in phrases so parallel to this section of 1 John that we can hardly escape the conclusion that the elder had the words of Jer 31 in mind.

> I will put my law within them, and I will write it upon their hearts; and I will be their God, and they shall be my people. And no longer shall each man teach his neighbor and each his brother, saying, "Know the Lord," for they shall all know me from the least of them to the greatest, says the Lord; for I will

> forgive their iniquity, and I will remember their sin no more (Jer 31:33–34 RSV).

Those who claim to know God must therefore have his laws inscribed on their hearts. Keeping God's commands is therefore evidence that we know him; and—equally true—if one does not keep God's commands, that person cannot claim to know God. The previous section of the epistle dealt with the forgiveness of sin, and the next section will address various groups in the community, from the least to the greatest. All of these concerns are related features of Jeremiah's vision of the new covenant, a covenant which the elder viewed as having been effected by the death of Jesus. His love and his words now abide in us, and we abide in him. Because each of these points will be important to the argument of 1 John, their common origin from Jeremiah needs to be noted.

Like the previous section, 1 John 2:3–11 contains three allusions to the claims of the elder's opponents. Rather than following the earlier pattern of relating these claims in conditional sentences, the author reports them using the formula "the one who claims. . . ."

> 2:4 The one who claims, "I know him," and is not keeping his commands . . .
> 2:6 The one who claims to abide in him . . .
> 2:9 The one who claims to be in the light and hates his brother . . .

The three claims are not in themselves false or objectionable. The elder might well make each of these claims for himself and those who follow his teachings. They know God, abide in him, and walk in the light. His point is that those who make such claims must show by their lives that they are speaking the truth.

Overconfidence is another subtle discipleship disease. The danger is not overconfidence in our fellowship with God but a confidence for which our lives give no evidence. Sermons on this section might deal with "Three Tests of Spiritual Health": (1) the test of obedience, (2) the new command, and (3) hatred and love. Alternatively, one might explore the three approaches to God suggested by these verses: knowing, abiding, and being.

Knowing God: The Test of Obedience (2:3–5)

Verse 3 states the theme that will be treated throughout this section (vss. 3–11). Keeping his commands is the sure test that we have come to know God. Throughout this section the elder drives home the demand that claims to know God or abide in him can be true only if the lives of those who make these claims reflect the obedience of covenant living. By implication we may gather that his opponents made precisely these claims but did not maintain a pattern of life acceptable to the elder. We will later need to ask what it was about their lives that he found unacceptable, but for now it is enough to see that vs. 3 welds together theology and ethics, the claims that one is saved and the claim of salvation upon one's life.

The phrase "and by this we know" occurs (with slight variations) nine times in 1 John (2:3, 5; 3:16, 19, 24; 4:2, 6, 13; 5:2). Whether the phrase refers to what precedes or what follows must be determined in each case by the context. In 2:3 the phrase obviously points ahead to the condition, "if we keep his commandments." When the phrase is repeated in vs. 5 it forms a frame for vss. 3–5 and recalls all that has been said in these verses. Verse 3 cannot therefore be treated simply as the topic sentence for all of vss. 3–11. By this framing and by the threefold repetition of the verb *to know* in vss. 3–5 (and not elsewhere in vss. 6–11), vs. 3 is tied to this smaller unit. The verb *to know* occurs first in the present tense, then in the perfect tense, so the phrase may properly be translated "and by this we know that we have come to know him."

Knowledge of God may come to persons in various ways: by mystical union with the Divine, by the mysteries of secret rites of initiation ceremonies, by visions, by the revelations of angels or divine men, by eating and drinking in cultic settings, by studying the contents of sacred writings, by membership in religious communities, by ecstatic experiences, or by the utterances of inspired prophets. How can a person know whether he or she knows God, or whether the claims of others are to be trusted? Perhaps more importantly, how can a person come to know and experience God fully? The simple, profound answer is "if we keep his commandments." Consistent with the religion of Israel, the elder declares that fellowship with God comes through living in covenant relationship with him; it comes in obedience.

Keep is a word with a peculiar double-edged meaning in the Johannine idiom. It occurs eighteen times in the Gospel of John and seven times in 1 John. When it is used with a personal object, it means to protect, defend, or preserve (John 17:11, 12, 15; 1 John 5:18). More frequently it is used in connection with Jesus' word (singular: John 8:51, 52, 55; 14:23; 15:20; 17:6; *1 John 2:5*), words (plural: John 14:24), and commandments (John 14:15, 21; 15:10; *1 John 2:3, 4; 3:22, 24; 5:3*). Note that five out of the seven times *keep* is used in 1 John it has "his commandments" as its object. "Keeping his commandments" would mean both that they be preserved, protected, guarded, interpreted, and taught (the work of the Johannine school) and—more importantly—that they be believed, obeyed, and observed as a pattern of life. Obedience, not enlightenment or theological sophistication, is both the means and the test of one's actual experience of God. The elder's demand is as mundane and pragmatic as it is profound and effective. Knowledge of God does not free us from the need for obedience. Only those who are obedient can know God, and those who come to know him will naturally and genuinely live by the commandments that actualize his grace in human communities.

In the Johannine writings *commandment* is used both in the singular and in the plural with little apparent difference in meaning. Although the Mosaic law may lie in the background, the central concern lies with the revelation that has come through Jesus' words. The Gospel of John maintains that Jesus gave to the disciples what he heard from the Father (John 8:40; 10:18; 13:34). Only two specific commandments are given in John, however: "believe in God, believe also in me" (John 14:1), and "love one another as I have loved you" (John 13:34; 15:12). These commandments are repeated in 1 John 3:23: "And this is his commandment, that we should believe in the name of his Son Jesus Christ and love one another, just as he commanded us."

These commands defined the center of the Johannine community's life, but they left the concrete expressions of belief and love, the perimeter of the community, undefined. The elder's opponents may well have thought that they were the

ones who were following these commands and that the elder
was refusing to believe in the divinity of Christ by affirming
that he became flesh and refusing to show Christian love by
his attitude toward them. The lack of more specific commandments freed the community from legalism but
threatened its life by the absence of structure and limits.
How can the church move in unity and unanimity without
clearly defined doctrines and codes of conduct? On the other
hand, how can the church have clarity in these matters without killing the very quality of life that comes from living
freely in the Spirit and in fellowship with God? The problem
facing the elder has continued to plague the church right up
to the present. There is a line in "The Sound of Music" that
puts it well: "How do you catch a moonbeam? How can you
hold it in your hand?" Are we always trying to catch the
moonbeam?

Abiding in God: The New Command (2:6–8)

The second reference to the claims of the opponents turns
to the obligations of those who claim fellowship with God—
"the one who claims to abide in him" (vs. 6). Again, there is
nothing wrong with the claim itself. *Abiding* or *remaining* is
an important ingredient in Johannine soteriology. In the
Gospel the first disciples come asking Jesus where he
"abides" (John 1:38). True to John's love for the ironic, the
eventual answer to their question is "If anyone loves me
and keeps my word, then my Father will love him and we
will come and make an abiding place with him" (John
14:23). He will abide in them: "Abide in me and I in you"
(John 15:4). Such mutual indwelling, however, was always
based on a believing response and keeping his words (e.g.,
John 15:7). Apart from these there could be no claim to
abide in him. The Johannine community of faith expected
two things of its members: (1) confession of faith even when
that meant being severed from family and synagogue, and
(2) a life-style consistent with the community's faith. That
life-style was now the source of dispute. What is required or
forbidden for a believer? What distinguishes an authenti-
cally Christian way of life? The Johannine church had little
moral teaching in its tradition—merely that they must keep
Jesus' words. That deficiency now left them without clear

codes or guidelines. Both sound theological foundations and specific ethical injunctions have their place. Without the latter, the elder appealed to the only pattern for Christian living for which he could claim authority: "Live as he lived." Imitate Jesus.

Before moving to the ethical imperative, however, one should recognize that the imperative is based on the experience of abiding in him. The imperative for ethical living grows out of the prior experience of fellowship with God through Jesus Christ. Disciplined ethical living may deepen that fellowship as our obedience and sacrifice become a participation in and extension of his, but it does not make such fellowship possible. On the other hand, fellowship with Christ is viewed here as continuous and dynamic, and the implication is that those who do not follow his pattern of life can have no fellowship with him.

That fellowship is characterized as *abiding*, which is not a concept that will appeal to many modern Christians. Task-oriented, activist, socially conscious, success-oriented church members will have little appreciation for the importance of *abiding* with its mystical and contemplative overtones. We are more concerned with doing than with being. Yet 1 John reminds us, at least implicitly, that the highest claim that can be made for one's life is that he or she abides in Christ. Then, as a result of that experience, the quality of one's life changes. The experience of Christ within becomes evident in the visible, exterior fabric of one's life—the activities, relationships, pursuits, and sacrifices which reveal one's inner self and ultimate values.

Ought is a term used sparingly in the Johannine writings (John 13:14; 19:7; 1 John 2:6; 3:16; 4:11; 3 John 8). In all of these instances an appeal is made to action which is mandated by a higher (or divine) command or example. The Jews say that according to the law Jesus ought to die (John 19:7). The other instances appeal to the example of Jesus in foot-washing (John 13:14) and laying down his life (1 John 3:16) or his command to love one another (1 John 2:6; 4:11; 3 John 8). The sense and force of obligation, therefore, arises from the awareness of what Christ has already done for his own. The compulsion is based on gratitude for grace, not fear or force.

Adverbs seldom carry theological significance, but in the Johannine writings *just as* draws comparisons which trace the course of revelation and lay bare the lines of authority: just as it is written; just as Jesus said or did; just as the Father to the Son, so Jesus did for the disciples or the disciples should do for others. These analogies display the bases for authority for the Johannine Christians. The authority of Scripture was retained, but to it was added the authority of Jesus' words, the events of his life, and the pattern of the Father's relationship to him and his relationship to his disciples. These all became acceptable bases upon which the church could build its theology and ethics. Where explicit commands were lacking, therefore, direction could be drawn from less explicit elements of the church's gospel tradition. Here, in vs. 6, the appeal is to Jesus' pattern of life. One who claims to abide in him ought to live ("walk") as he lived. No more self-evident norm could be adduced, but the norm is so general that it does not convey to us exactly the manner of conduct it was intended to censure. It was therefore probably also open to debate by the elder's opponents. Were they not living as he had? How could anyone live exactly as he did? Since he was the unique Son, must not his life have been equally singular, a pattern not viable for his followers?

Verse 7 should be read as the continuation of vs. 6, with no paragraph division separating them. What the elder has in mind, above all, is the love which Jesus showed for his own and which he commanded for them. Because he was drawing authority from the pattern of Jesus' life, perhaps more explicitly than the community had previously, he may well have feared that his opponents would charge that he was imposing an innovative, new ethic upon them. To defend against such a charge, he claims that this is not a new command but one which they had from "the beginning." It is the word which they had heard. As noted in the discussion of 1:1, 1 John's references to the beginning may refer either to the days of Jesus' ministry or to the origin of the Johannine church. Here both senses may be intended. It is the command which Jesus gave and which was taught to new converts from the earliest days of the church. Its authority is therefore beyond dispute. *Word* and *command* are used interchangeably in 1 John. To the Ten Words of the Decalogue

Jesus had added an eleventh. "The word which you heard" is therefore both an old command and the new command. The tangled "double-talk" of vss. 7 and 8 arises from the given that the Gospel calls the command "new," but the elder must affirm that the command he places upon the community is not a recent development but one embedded in its heritage.

Jesus had said it was a new command (John 13:34), and it is new in the sense that it is *the* command of the new covenant which gives order to the community of disciples. It is made new, moreover, by the death of Jesus, laying down his life, which transforms the relationship between God and the people of the new covenant. The relative clause in vs. 8 is difficult because the gender of the relative pronoun is neuter, not feminine as one would expect if the antecedent is "a new commandment." The change of gender, along with the change of subject in the last half of vs. 8, may indicate that the writer's thought is moving toward more general considerations of the new effects of Christ's redemptive work. Whatever the precise antecedent of the relative clause (the new commandment, the newness, the new covenant, or the revelation and new order effected by Jesus), it is true or genuine, grounded in the ultimate reality of God's character as it is revealed in both Jesus Christ and the community of believers.

God's love—revealed and conveyed by Jesus, extended through the new commandment, and realized in the community—is both the force driving out darkness and evidence that the new age has come. The command's newness, therefore, is eschatological also. In Johannine symbolism, darkness represents the order of life which is closed to the revelation of God in Jesus. The darkness cannot overcome the light (John 1:5), however. Indeed, the light is already shining. Jesus himself is the true light (2:8; John 1:9), and his redemptive work has borne fruit in the new order of life represented by the Johannine community.

Being in the Light: Hatred and Love (2:9–11)

The third false claim arises out of the language of vs. 8. It also forms the climax to 2:3–11. The progression of thought is apparent in the claims: the one who claims to know God (2:4), to abide in him (2:6), to be in the light (2:9). Knowing

God enables one to abide in him. Those who abide in him live in the light. Again, the author of the Epistles would agree with the logic of this claim, but he challenges the hypocrisy of those who claim to be in the light yet do not live by the new commandment.

We do not know how much may have been intended by the claim of the opponents to be in the light. They may have been claiming communion with God or Christ, a higher quality of spiritual enlightenment by virtue of sharing divine knowledge, or simply partnership with the Johannine community. The phrase *to be in* occurs in the infinitive form only here in 1 John, but it is prepared for by earlier references: "we walk in the darkness" (1:6), "as he is in the light" (1:7), and "we are in him" (2:5). Such a claim, however, is disallowed for any who do not love their fellow Christians, members of the same community. 1 John does not extend the duty of love to one's enemies or to all human beings; it focuses narrowly on the new commandment, that Christians love one another. They are *brothers* in the sense that they are now all children of God through faith in the unique Son of God (see John 1:12; 20:17; 21:23). By their refusal to love members of the Johannine community, the opponents show that they are still in the darkness—like Judas (John 13:30). The author may also imply that they love the darkness rather than the light (see John 3:19). Remaining in the light requires imitation of Christ, at least through obedience to the new command.

Verse 10 states a related axiom: if one loves his brother, he abides in the light. Such love within the community is genuine evidence of knowledge of God and fellowship with Christ. Through their fellowship with the community of faith, such believers show that they are a part of the light which entered the world in Christ and has been transforming it ever since. The elder may in fact have been a forerunner of Cyprian, the church father of the third century who claimed that outside the church there could be no salvation.

In those who practice love for the community there is no offense. If this is the meaning of the latter part of vs. 10, then the elder is moving toward absolutizing the ethic of fraternal love as the standard by which believers will be judged. On the other hand, his words probably have a much more practi-

cal objective. They affirm that those who love within the
Christian community are above reproach and drive out unbelief, hatred, and sin. The active sense of the Greek *skandalon*
may also apply: such believers will not cause others to stum-
ble or draw them away from the community.

Verse 11 returns to the attack on those who do not love the
Christian community. The opposite of love is not lack of love
but hatred. Those who do not love their fellow Christians,
therefore, hate them. They are in the darkness, like Judas,
alienated from the fellowship gathered around Christ and
controlled instead by the power of evil. All that they do is
determined by the power of darkness within them. Far from
knowing God, they do not even know where they are going.
They do not realize what the end of their journey will be. The
tragic irony is that the darkness to which they have given
themselves has blinded them. Such is the destructive power
of the darkness.

This section of the letter serves the very practical purpose
of holding up all our claims and the claims of others to the
test of whether our relationship to the church and to other
believers reflects Christlike love. It forms an indissoluble
bond between confession and community living which can
serve again and again to forge authenticity for our confessions and theological significance for our efforts to live
Christlike lives. The elder's word is both a promise and a
demand: if we live in fellowship with Christ, then his love
will be at work within us, enabling us to love as he loved,
extending ever further his redemptive work, and giving light
to those still blinded by the darkness of their pursuits.

Victory Assured, Resistance Required
(1 John 2:12–17)

Having responded to the false claims of the opponents, the elder now encourages the community of the faithful by assuring them that the benefits of the new covenant are theirs and warns them against the dangers that remain. This section falls naturally into two parts: 2:12–14, exhortation to three groups which constitute the community, and 2:15–17, admonition that resistance is still required.

Taken together these two paragraphs balance assurance and challenge, proclamation and exhortation. They characterize the dynamic tension of Christian experience: believers experience the forgiveness of sin, victory over temptation, and a taste of that quality of life which is open to those who know God. On the other hand, the struggle continues. Those forces which threaten Christian experience and community are strong and lie dangerously close at hand. Persistent resistance is required, but the armor and weapons of the Christian include the abiding presence of God through his word.

The Family of God (2:12–14)

In vss. 12–14 the writer breaks out in two stanzas of assurance which are almost poetic in structure. Patterns of three predominate. Verses 12–13 contain three statements, each beginning "I write to you. . . ." Verse 14 repeats the pattern in a different tense, "I have written to you. . . ." In both stanzas three groups are mentioned: children, fathers, young men. For all the apparent simplicity of these verses, they present difficulties which have troubled scribes and commentators from the earliest centuries. What significance has the change of tenses? Why does the author repeat the same basic affirmations in the second stanza? Who are the children, fathers, and young men? Finally, should the Greek word *hoti* be interpreted as declarative ("that") or causative ("because")?

Although these difficulties may elude final resolution, the

interpreter or preacher is on safest ground when choosing
the alternatives which best fit the historical situation of the
epistle. The elder is writing to faithful members of the Johannine community who have not been led astray by those who
have gone out from them. The danger posed by this schism
compels the elder to write to the community exposing and
answering the false claims of the defectors and encouraging
the community to remain faithful to the tradition and teaching they had received from the beginning, from those who
knew Jesus. The use of the present and aorist tenses in these
verses may therefore intend to convey that what the elder is
writing, and all that the Johannine school has written, is consistent with these basic affirmations. If such is the case, the
translation of *hoti* as "that" is to be preferred over the causal
translation. The elder is not writing to the community *because* these things are true; he writes to assure them in the
face of opposition that they indeed are the ones who have
been forgiven, who know the Christ, and who have overcome
the evil one.

The most vexing problem is the identity of the "children,"
"fathers," and "young men." C. H. Dodd pointed out that the
privileges mentioned here belong to all Christians. He argued, therefore, that the three are not meant to address individual age groups but are rather a rhetorical figure for
addressing the whole community. Others have adopted the
"three age groups" interpretation, but the sequence—children, fathers, young men—does not fit a chronological
scheme. A third alternative emerges when one recognizes
that the address "children" recurs repeatedly in the Johannine writings. Two terms for children are used in these
verses: *teknia* (vs. 12) and *paidia* (vs. 14). The first is characteristically Johannine, and is Jesus' form of address to the
disciples when he gave the new commandment (which was
the subject of the preceding verses). See the references cited
above in the discussion of 2:1. The second term is used less
frequently as a designation for disciples or believers but
seems to carry the same meaning (John 21:5; 1 John 2:14,
18). The alternative between the two terms is probably
merely stylistic.

The main point to be drawn from the use of these terms is
that readers could have been expected to recognize that

when the elder addressed *children* he was writing to the entire community, the children of God, children for whom the elder had responsibility. But what of the other two terms, *fathers* and *young men*? Do these terms denote emerging offices in the Johannine church more or less comparable to the elders and deacons of the Pauline churches, or are they representative references for the older and younger or more and less mature Christians in the community? Jeremiah wrote in the words of the new covenant, "For they shall all know me, from the least of them to the greatest" (31:34, RSV). Joel wrote that the young men would see visions (2:28), and there is some evidence that the early church took over the distinction between young men (Acts 2:17; 5:10; and perhaps also the Gospel references Mark 14:51; 16:5) and elders (compare also Titus 2:2–8). These verses may therefore be viewed as a Johannine appropriation of a form of the household code of ethical standards (known from Eph 5:21—6:9; Col 3:18—4:1; 1 Peter 2:18—3:7).

The words are appropriate for all Christians: "your sins are forgiven on account of his name" (vs. 12) and "you have known the Father" (vs. 14). There is again a direct correspondence between these claims and the provisions of the new covenant, "they shall all know me ... for I will forgive their iniquity, and I will remember their sin no more" (Jer 31:34, RSV). Verse 12 may have its home in a baptismal context. It sounds much like an early kerygmatic assurance which could have been pronounced when one was baptized. If so, these were again words they had heard "from the beginning." Baptism was first practiced "in the name of Jesus" (Acts 2:38; 10:48). For the Johannine community, *the name* had power, derived from the person of Jesus (John 1:12; 3:18; 15:21; 16:23; 17:11; 20:31; 1 John 3:23; 5:15; 3 John 7). The assurance that they knew God was also fundamental to the Johannine understanding of salvation. The parenthesis in John 17 declares, "And this is eternal life, that they know thee the only true God, and Jesus Christ whom thou hast sent" (17:3, RSV). No more significant assurance could be given to the community than that they were the ones who had come to know God. Such an affirmation stripped the threat from any rival religious system. Because the faithful knew God, no higher teaching could be given to them. Knowing God be-

stows the highest privilege, the grace of his fellowship, and
the possibility of living a life already filled with the eternal
qualities which belong to that fellowship.

Except for the change in tense, the second element is iden-
tical in both stanzas: "I write (have written) to you, fathers,
that you have known the one who has been from the beginning" (2:13a, 14b). The affirmation may be particularly appropriate to the "fathers" if they are the elder members of
the community. Both the ambiguity and the rich allusions of
the phrase "the one who has been from the beginning" are
typically Johannine. The first lines of the Gospel and the
epistle echo in the reader's memory. Christ is the one who
was present in the beginning of time, in the beginning of his
incarnation and ministry, and in the beginning of the church.
As senior members of the community, the fathers had come
to know the earthly Jesus through the eyewitness tradition of
the Beloved Disciple, which was preserved by the Johannine
community. The stabilizing tradition of the Gospels and the
church is an important aspect of how each generation can
come to know the one who stands at the beginning of that
tradition. The knowledge in question, therefore, is not necessarily a personal, eyewitness acquaintance but the more significant experience which results from one self having been
open to another, changing the other's entire perception of
life. While the "fathers" may guarantee the continuing possibility of such knowledge, it is also available to the "children"
and "young men" of each new generation.

The first stanza ends with the assurance that the "young
men" have overcome the evil one (2:13b). The second stanza
picks up this assurance but develops it into a three-mem-
bered conclusion for the entire sequence: (1) "you are
strong," (2) "the word of God abides in you," and (3) "you
have overcome the evil one." Given the sharp dualism of
Johannine thought, there could be no peaceful coexistence.
The cosmic struggle between the two spheres of existence—
good and evil, light and darkness, truth and falsehood, love
and hate, life and death, God and the devil, Christ and the
antichrists, the community and the world—had to be resolved in the victory of one over the other. The assurance of
victory, therefore, is a characteristic element of the Johannine Gospel. Rejoicing is in order because Christ has over-

come the world (John 16:33). By extension, our faith has conquered the world (1 John 5:4), and victory over the world belongs to those who believe that Jesus is the Son of God (4:4; 5:5). The theme of victory also pervades the book of Revelation, where the verb "to conquer" appears seventeen times.

The world lies under the power of evil, "the ruler of this world" (John 12:31; 16:11), and can therefore characterize all that is opposed to Christ. The ruler has been judged and cast out, but the antichrists, false prophets, liars, murderers, and those who would deceive the children of God continue, if only for a little while. The community is called to resist, but the "young men" are strong. The conclusion (vs. 14) explains the basis of their strength: they have the word of God abiding in them. That word is also pictured in martial images in the Bible. It is sharper than any two-edged sword (Heb 4:12; Rev 1:16). The sword of the Spirit is the word of God (Eph 6:17). In 1 John that word is above all the revelation of the Father through Jesus, which is the core of the gospel. His is the liberating word which is uniquely able to convey knowledge of the truth, freedom, and final deliverance from the power of evil.

The language of Christian warfare may sound quaint and medieval to modern ears; who but religious fanatics and kooks take up the word of God in battle against the devil? The struggle for justice, peace, and righteousness seldom offers battlefields where the lines are so clearly drawn. On the other hand, the polar alternatives with which the Johannine writings sketch the world should remind all of us who perceive the world in grays and shadows from the soft, indirect lighting of our comfortable dwellings that there are serious moral alternatives, alternatives which can make differences between life and death. The gospel, therefore, does not allow neutrality. Commitment to Christ demands that we participate in the struggle to establish his sovereignty in the world in which we live.

Sermons on these verses may emphasize the role of the church as that of a family (a needed emphasis in a time when the disruption of families is so common) or the assurances the elder pronounces (as an antidote to pervasive skepticism and uncertainty). On the other hand, the language of warfare in these verses can lend itself well to a sermon on "A Cause Worth Fighting For."

Aggressive Resistance (2:15–17)

The second part of this section exhorts the community to resist the world. Each of the three verses draws a contrast:

2:15—The love of the Father vs. the love of the world

2:16—That which is from the Father vs. that which is from the world

2:17—The world which is passing away vs. the will which abides forever

The first verse exposes the opposition of conflicting loves, the second details the origin and nature of the two loves, and the third contrasts the ends of the opposing powers.

Verse 15 begins with a negative imperative, "Do not love the world or the things in the world," and concludes by drawing the consequences of disobeying the command; the love of the Father is not in such people. Two questions arise: how should this prohibition be related to John's declaration that God loved the world (John 3:16), and what provoked the elder to write in this way? If God loves the world, why should the Christian not love the world? It is difficult to escape the conclusion that we are dealing with different concepts of love or different concepts of the world in John 3:16 and 1 John 2:15. *Love* can mean either desiring the best for someone else to the point of self-sacrifice, or merely intense desire for the object of one's love. Similarly, *the world* in John 3:16 seems to encompass all human life, while in 1 John 2:15 it represents all that is opposed to Christ (as in John 17:9). The phrase, "the love of the Father," may be taken either subjectively (the Father's love) or objectively (love for the Father). The two cannot be sharply distinguished, however, since the elder will later maintain that our capacity to love God derives from his love for us.

Were the elder's opponents guilty of lust, greed, and worldly concerns, or had they merely so given themselves to their mission to the world that they neglected love for the Father and the community of believers? The issue is difficult both because the elder uses invective to condemn positions

he rejects and because the meaning of the metaphorical language in 2:16 is open to different nuances. Raymond Brown
advances the latter position in his definitive commentary on
these epistles. In his favor are the later passages which con-
nect the false prophets with the world: they have gone out
into the world (4:1; 2 John 7); and they are from the world,
speak from the world, and the world hears them (4:5). These
vague descriptions imply that the false prophets, having left
the community (2:19), met with success in drawing others to
their beliefs. The elder condemns these defectors from the
community by saying that they and their ways belong to the
sphere of the unredeemed world.

Verse 16 explains *the things* that belong to the world, using
language that had become commonplace in Jewish and
Christian ethical teachings. The list of three phrases is characteristically unbalanced: (a) the desire of the flesh, (b) the
desire of the eyes, and (c) the pride of life. The third member
alters the pattern while remaining clearly the last in this sequence of phrases, which sound like clichés.

Desire, or lust, is used only twice in the Johannine writings
outside this passage: once in the Gospel, where it is connected with the devil (John 8:44), and once in Revelation,
where the destruction of the merchants and their wares is
described (Rev 18:14). Early Christian ethical instruction,
which may also have been used in the instruction of new converts, often connected *desire* and *flesh* (Gal 5:16, 24; 1 Peter
2:11; 2 Peter 2:10, 18). In the Johannine writings *flesh* does
not necessarily have sinful or sexual connotations. The confession the elder requires is that Jesus Christ came *in flesh* (1
John 4:2; 2 John 7). On the other hand, "the will of flesh" is
contrasted with the Father's will (John 1:13), flesh is set in
opposition to spirit (John 3:6; 6:63), and judging according to
the flesh is false, unenlightened judgment (John 8:15). Flesh,
therefore, characterizes the natural, human order; and "the
desire of the flesh" means all that the unredeemed human
will craves.

Eyes are often associated with lust and greed in the OT and
in Jewish and Christian materials. In John, however, the recurring theme is that Jesus opened blind eyes (John 9), and
the judgment of Isaiah is repeated:

He has blinded their eyes
    and hardened their heart,
lest they should see with their eyes
    and perceive with their heart,
and turn for me to heal them (John 12:40, RSV; Isa 6:10).

The "desire of the eyes" in this context is thereby scarcely distinguishable in meaning from the previous phrase—the unenlightened, and therefore sinful, desires of the human heart.

The third phrase breaks the pattern of the first two by not using *desire*. Its meaning is only slightly different, however. The term often translated by *pride* occurs elsewhere in the NT only in James 4:16, "You boast in your arrogance. All such boasting is evil." It is presumption or overconfidence, the attitude to which the successful and self-sufficient easily fall prey. Arrogance is blind to its own faults and vulnerability. *Life (bios)* here is not the life *(zoe)* which derives from Christ (John 1:4) and is promised to those who believe (John 10:10; 20:31). It is rather the natural life of the world order or the goods and means of life (1 John 3:17). To be arrogant or presumptuous over the life or goods of the unenlightened, therefore, is a further characteristic of those who love this world rather than love the Father. When understood in these terms, this verse bites deep into the soft underbelly of the materialism of American Christianity.

The two loves cannot be reconciled. One comes from the Father, the other from the world. In Johannine thought one does not escape one's origins: to be "from" the world is always to "belong to" the world. The only hope of escape is a new beginning, a new birth, "from above" (John 3:3).

Verse 17 contrasts the outcomes of these two loves, two lives, and two orientations toward Life. Christ has overcome the world (John 16:33). The world and its darkness (1 John 2:8) are therefore *passing away*. This verse recalls the apocalyptic hopes of early Christianity (Mark 13:31; 1 Cor 7:29, 31), but the verb can also be used in a metaphorical sense. The old order has been transcended and is passing away (2 Cor 5:17; 8:13; Rev 21:4–5).

The transitory world order provides a contrast to the enduring life of those who belong to the Christian community:

"the one who does the will of God abides forever" (2:17b).
Each element in the second half of the verse has a counterpart in the first half: the obedient versus the world, the will
of God versus the desire of the world, and "abides for ever"
versus "passes away." To do the will of God is to be obedient
to him, just as Jesus was. According to John, Jesus did not
seek his own will but that of his Father, who had sent him
(John 5:30; 6:38–40). Doing the Father's will is the very food
which sustains the new life (John 4:34). The believer, therefore, is to live as Jesus lived. Obedience to God's will is surely
a part of obeying Jesus' commands and keeping his word,
which were discussed earlier (1 John 2:3–5). Those who do
the Father's will know the teaching that is from God (John
7:17); they will be heard by God (John 9:31); and they will be
given eternal life and raised on the last day (John 6:39, 40).
The final and ultimate assurance to the community, therefore, is that they will "remain forever." They already enjoy a
fellowship with God which will transcend this life and endure throughout his eternity. This assurance too is deeply
rooted in traditional Johannine theology (John 4:14; 6:51, 58;
8:51–52; 10:28; 11:26; 14:16).

For all its dualistic and idiomatic language, this section
conveys both a powerful promise to the church and a realis-
tic warning against the danger of easy compromise with the
pursuits of the secular economy in which we live. Living according to the knowledge of God and the example of Christ is
set in opposition to the desires and ambitions which come
naturally even to those who struggle to know what it means
to be in the world but not of it (John 17:11, 16). Both emphases are needed. The church needs to be reminded of its for-
eignness because compromise with the society in which it
lives is a persistent threat. Assurance of God's ability to preserve his own will come as living water to those who fear
annihilation by cancer, heart disease, or nuclear cataclysm.
Understood in context and translated into contemporary idiom, these paragraphs will continue to capture for the
church both the essence of the good news and the ethic required of those who receive it.

Sermons on this section should embrace both emphases:
victory is assured, resistance is required.

The Nature of Deception
(1 John 2:18–27)

1 John as a whole can be interpreted as a warning against deception. The elder was locked in conflict with another group, which apparently emerged from the Johannine community but taught a different doctrine. In this section more than any other, the elder writes specifically about the opposing movement, which had divided the community. The division is the first recorded schism in the history of the church— the beginning of a tragic but seemingly inescapable by-product of Christian *koinonia*. Throughout, the elder warns the faithful of the danger of being misled by deviant teachings. In this section of the letter he lays bare the nature of deception, and in doing so passes on to every generation of believers a study in the dangers, origin, and effects of the counterfeit teachings which constantly threaten to destroy the church. Try adapting this material to a sermon on "Faith's Counterfeits."

This section can be seen as an outgrowth of the previous one, which encouraged adherence to the core of the gospel they had received and resistance to the corrupting influence of the unredeemed world. The community had not been able to avoid those destructive influences, however, so the elder turns to the specific threat which has already led a number of their fellowship astray: the false teachings of the opponents.

While the beginning, ending, and internal structure of the previous units have been relatively clear, the ending of the present section is debated, and its internal structure is not obvious. Commentators and translations which divide the text into paragraphs have been fairly evenly split over whether vs. 28 constitutes the end of this section or the beginning of the next. The parallels with vs. 18 are clear: a reference to "children" (*paidia* in vs. 18, *teknia* in vs. 28), a temporal reference ("the last hour," "now"), and the coming of the antichrists (vs. 18) versus the coming of Christ (vs. 28). The question is whether vs. 28 forms a frame for the section which begins at vs. 18 or marks the introduction of the next section. Since the coming of Christ is central to the next section (2:28—3:10), vs. 28 is probably better seen as the introduction to what follows it. Transitional verses which have links with both the preceding and the following sections are common in 1 John.

Within 2:18–27 the preacher will find a series of three contrasts between the faithful and their opponents:

2:18	Introduction: The appearance of antichrists proves that it is the last hour.
	1. Schism reveals those who belong to the truth and those who do not.
2:19	The antichrists went out from us.
2:20–21	You have an anointing and know the truth.
	2. You have the confession of Christ; the others deny him.
2:22–23	Liars and antichrists deny that Jesus is the Christ.
2:24–25	Abide in the confession which you have had from the beginning.
	3. You have an anointing which teaches you; they are deceivers.
2:26	I have written to expose the deceivers.
2:27	You do not need their teaching; abide in the anointing you have received.

This structuring of the section into three units results from observing that there are three emphatic addresses to the readers, to "you," in vss. 20, 24, and 27. Each address marks a contrast to the description of the opponents in the preceding verse or verses. The first and third units mention the anointing of the faithful. The second unit emphasizes their confession. Where there are two verses per element, the second verse (21, 23, 25) functions as a clarification or comment on the previous verse. A sermon on these verses could describe the qualities of authentic Christian teachings and might help believers distinguish genuine teachings from the bizarre assortment of religious pronouncements carried in the popular media today.

The Hour of the Antichrists (2:18)

The single theme of this introductory verse is that the last hour has come because antichrists have appeared. The word for "children" is the same one used in 2:14 and 3:7 (*paidia*). The address and the introduction of two new themes, the last hour and the antichrists, signal the beginning of a new section. Both of these new terms are unique to the Johannine Epistles. Since they do not occur anywhere earlier and appear only here in the NT, both terms *the last hour* and *antichrist* (1 John 2:18, 22; 4:3; 2 John 7) were apparently coined by the Johannine community. Neither term, however, is without antecedents in the OT and early Christian writings.

The article is not used with *last hour*, but the definiteness and finality of the adjective make it impossible to think that the writer intended to say merely that "a last hour" had come. The OT and the Qumran Scrolls refer frequently to "the last days," and in the Synoptics Jesus speaks of "that hour." The Gospel of John promises the resurrection of the believers at "the last day" (John 6:39, 40, 44, 54; 11:24; 12:48). The day of resurrection is also described as an hour (John 5:25, 28). Jesus promises the coming of an hour when the disciples would be killed (John 16:2; see 16:25). The ministry of Jesus marked the coming of an hour (John 4:21, 23), and the approach of "the hour" of his death and exaltation builds suspense in the Gospel of John. Now "the last hour" had come.

Jewish and early Christian apocalyptic literature vividly describes the horrors that would precede the final vindication of the faithful. Drawing from the treasury of this literature, the book of Revelation states that the end will be marked by the appearance of evil rulers, beasts, false prophets, and Satan. Sketching the opponents in the darkest colors possible and raising the sense of crisis, the elder coins new terms related to traditional apocalyptic language. Those who have left the community are "antichrists"; their appearance shows that the terrors of the last days have already begun.

The elder's choice of language is effective, if nevertheless dangerous. It has fired imaginations and provided a precedent for turning the language of judgment of the wicked upon other believers with whom one disagrees. That bloody trail can be followed from 1 John through the Reformation to the sectarian and divisive fundamentalist movements of the present. It takes perception and sensitivity to distinguish between tolerable differences and intolerable deviations or to recognize the difference between the appropriation of traditional beliefs in new forms and the departure from essential doctrines for the sake of innovation or relevance. Perhaps it takes even more prophetic wisdom to know when schism is preferable to compromise. Modern Christians can probably learn more from 1 John about the dangers of branding others with such sharp epithets than about the need to recognize heresy when it appears in others. The danger which faced the Johannine community was the possibility of being led astray by failure to recognize the implications of certain contemporary teachings. The more urgent danger to the church today is that it may be wrecked by hypersensitivity to the need for "pure" doctrine.

The First Schism (2:19–21)

Because the first readers of this epistle would have been familiar with the current situation in the community, little is said about the events which led to the schism. 1 John 2:19 confirms that a part of the community separated from it, but does not tell us how or why. Other passages (for example, 4:1–2) suggest that the issue was primarily christological, that is, it concerned the interpretation of Jesus in Christian faith. We do not know whether the group that left was a majority or a small minority, nor whether their leaving was formal or forced, though we may conjecture that it was simply the result of differences leading to open confrontation and sharp exchanges, resulting in a broken fellowship and severed relations. Inevitably, some did not see the issues as clearly as others or were on the verge of leaving the community to join the other group. The elder, therefore, writes as a leader of the community—probably one who had been associated with the Beloved Disciple—to set forth the differences sharply, to brand the departing group as antichrists belonging to the world, to charge them with betrayal and disobedience to the command to love the brethren, and thereby to encourage unity among those who remained. Resisting the corrupting influence of the world (2:15–17) meant specifically resisting the group that had left the community (2:18–19).

The language used in these verses is typically Johannine

and describes the exodus from the elder's point of view. Note the language of division in vs. 19: *they* (six times) and *us* (five times, four times in the phrase *from us*). When members of a church or denomination begin to speak of *we* and *they*, that body is already descending the well-worn path toward schism. Differences have already resulted in polarization and the kind of subgroup mentality which makes vindicating one's views and defeating the other group more important than reestablishing unity in the fellowship.

The elder implicitly lays the blame on the other group: "*They* went out from us." The implication that the other group was responsible for breaking relations and thereby disobeying the covenant command to love one another is driven home both by charging them with leaving and by the associations which "going out" may have had in the Johannine community. In the Gospel, Judas and the Galilean defectors "went out" from the disciples who remained with Jesus (John 6:66–67; 13:30–31). Like Judas, therefore, the other group went out from the community of light into the darkness of the world (4:1). Because they did not remain with the community, they showed that they did not love the brethren. Therefore, they "hate" their brothers, show that the darkness has blinded their eyes (2:11), and do not know where they are going.

The phrase *from us* is repeated four times in vs. 19, and the author plays on its meanings. They went out "from us," but they were not "from us." In each case except the first, "from us" carries the sense that they did not belong to us. They were from the world, not from God (4:4–6), and origin indicates identity and belonging. If they were not "from us," even though they went out from the community, then they were never "of us"; they did not belong in the community.

The elder's reasoning is circular, but impeccable given his assumptions. If they had really been a part of the community, children of God, then they would have remained "with us." The community was abiding in fellowship with Christ through the Spirit, so if the others had belonged to Christ also, they would have remained in the community.

Their leaving can be seen in retrospect as having occurred to reveal who they really were. *Reveal* or "make manifest" (*phaneroo*) is used in the Johannine writings to describe the disclosure of spiritual realities: the Baptist came to reveal the Christ to Israel (John 1:31), the miracle at Cana revealed Jesus' glory (John 2:11), his brothers challenged Jesus to reveal himself to the world (John 7:4), Jesus healed the blind man to reveal God's works (John 9:3), and the risen Lord manifested himself to the disciples in his appearances (John 21:1, 14). In him Life (1 John 1:2) and the love of God (1 John 4:9) were manifest, and the *parousia* will reveal both Christ and us as his children (1 John 2:28; 3:2). The revelation of the true identity of the defectors was therefore a part of the eschatological sifting and disclosure of the last hour.

The last part of vs. 19 poses grammatical difficulties. It can mean either "not all of them belong to us" or "none of them belongs to us." The latter sense depends on recognizing the Greek construction which negates *all* to mean *none*. In this instance the negative particle, *not*, negates the entire phrase which follows it and yields the sense which we would expect. Because they all "went out from us," not one of them belongs to us.

Verse 20 affirms the faithful. The contrast with those who have gone out is shown by the anointing which the community has received. The term *anointing* occurs only here in the NT (2:20, 27). Either it may refer to a physical act of anointing, probably at baptism, or it may have a more figurative meaning. Probably it carries the sense that upon entering the community believing in Christ as the Son of God, each of them was "anointed" with the Holy Spirit. At least the functions of this anointing accord well with the Fourth Gospel's allusions to the work of the Paraclete which would abide with them and teach them all things. Alternatively, some commentators take the anointing as a reference to the word of God which they heard from the beginning (see vs. 24). *The holy one* from whom they have received the anointing is probably Christ. The anointing is therefore from the anointed one, the chrism (*chrisma*) from the Christ (*christos*).

A textual variant clouds the meaning of the last clause in vs. 20. The manuscripts are divided, but the favored and more difficult reading is "you all have knowledge." The alternative is "you know all things." The elder is assuring the faithful that they are the ones who have knowledge of the truth, that Jesus is the Christ (2:21–22). That is the object of their knowledge, and his insistence that they all have knowl-

edge of God again echoes the words of the new covenant in
Jer 31:34, "they shall all know me."

Verse 21 clarifies what the elder has just written. It is not
that the community does not know the truth and needs the
elder to convey it to them. On the contrary, because they
have the anointing of the Spirit they do know the truth.
Neither the theology nor the polity of the Johannine church
would allow the elder to claim authority to dispense or dictate truth to the community. This verse contains three *hoti*
clauses which may be translated either as *that* or as *because*.
Most translations render at least the first two as *because*
(KJV, RSV, TEV, NEB), but the pastoral assurance is conveyed
better by taking all three as meaning *that*: "I have not written to you that you do not know the truth but that you know
it and that no lie is from the truth." This interpretation is
favored by many recent commentators (Brown, Bultmann,
de la Potterie, Marshall, Schnackenburg). The last assertion
reflects the Johannine dualism; nothing false can come from
the truth. The two spheres, truth and falsehood, are totally
and distinctly separate, even if they do not always appear so.

The Christian's Confession (2:22–25)

Christians who enjoy the goodwill of the society and state
in which they live can hardly appreciate the trauma and sacrifice confession requires where Christians are persecuted.
The Gospel of John, however, reflects a context of conflict
with the synagogue. Confessing that Jesus was the Christ
could mean separation from family and expulsion from the
Jewish community (see John 9:22; 16:2). In such a setting the
confession toward which the Gospel draws its readers, "that
Jesus is the Christ, the Son of God" (John 20:31; see 11:27),
could have caused a believer to be ostracized by family, un-
employed, and excluded from the subgroup which gave identity and protection to Jews in major cities of the Roman
Empire. Confession was therefore the distinctive mark of the
believer and would have had an important place in whatever
ceremony marked the initiation of a believer into the Christian community. It is not surprising, then, that John opens
with the solemn affirmation that John the Baptist "confessed, he did not deny, but confessed" (1:20). Later, Peter's
unwillingness to be identified as a follower of Jesus is
branded as "denying" Jesus, a description we might find sur-

prising if it were not so familiar to us (John 13:28; 18:25, 27). The elder now identifies one who denies Jesus as "the liar" (1 John 2:22).

Verse 22 is the only place in the Johannine writings where *liar* is used with the article, as a title or designation of a known figure. The Gospel of John brands as a liar both the devil and anyone who claims to know God but refuses to accept his revelation of himself in Jesus (8:44, 55). Characteristically, the elder takes the polemical language of the Gospel and directs it toward those who departed from the community. For Johannine readers, using the definite article with *liar* probably suggested that the elder meant the devil. Consequently, all who denied that Jesus is the Christ are seen as belonging to the devil.

Was this a general condemnation of all unbelievers? Probably not. Although such a condemnation might be expected as an extension of the elder's warning against loving the world or anything that pertains to it (2:15–17), the object of this epistle's polemics is more narrowly defined. Coming as it does just after the specific reference in 2:19, we have all the more reason to expect that this contrasting of confession and denial is aimed at those who have gone out from the community. Is it conceivable, though, that they would have refused to make the distinctive confession that Jesus is the Christ? All who had joined the Johannine community would have made this confession upon entering the community, and there is no evidence that those who left had denied their Christian beliefs entirely. More likely is the suggestion that the elder is evoking the most familiar Christian confession and implying that by leaving the community his opponents had abandoned their earlier confession, thereby "denying" Jesus. As so often occurs in controversies between segments of the Christian community, both parties were probably appealing to the accepted authorities, confessions, or codes and charging, either explicitly or by innuendo, that the others opposed some essential element of the Christian faith. At this distance it is probably impossible to reconstruct the specifics of the opponents' beliefs, but the elder's demand later in the letter that believers must confess Jesus "who came in the flesh" (4:2) gives us some reason to think that the opponents maintained the divinity of Jesus as the creating and revealing *logos* but denied that he had actually become a

human being "anointed" by God—the Christ. This difference
in Christology had probably provoked the controversy which
resulted in one group's severing relations with the other.

The second half of vs. 22 and all of vs. 23 answer the rhetorical question raised in the first part of vs. 22 and clarify
its implications. "The liar" is "the antichrist." The allusion
in code words connects earlier references. The "antichrists"
who have come in the last hour are those who have gone out
from the community. They are "liars" and belong to "the
liar," the devil and the antichrist, who "denies" both the
Father and the Son. By this sequence of identifications the
elder unmasks his opponents. The logic is as simple and effective as it is dangerous: those who abandon the core confession of the Christian faith reject Christ and show that
they belong to the devil. Only those who fear that the Christian faith is being destroyed from within and are therefore
willing to suffer division of the church will level such
charges against others who also claim to belong to Christ.
But had the elder shrunk from making these charges, the
affirmation of the incarnation might have been lost; the
church's confession might have been stated in less potent,
less profound terms.

Verse 23 draws a further implication. Since Jesus is "the
way, and the truth, and the life" and "no one comes to the
Father" except through him (John 14:6), one who denies the
Son cannot claim to have the Father. "Having the Father"
belongs only to those who confess the Son. Confession, we
may gather, must be public (see John 12:42), in the context
of initiation and worship in the Christian community.
"Having the Father" presumably meant sharing in his legacy to the "children of God": light, love, peace, joy, eternal
life, the word of God, and the love of God. Those who
claimed mystical union or an elevated knowledge of God
could not share in this legacy apart from confessing that
Jesus was the Christ.

Verse 24 returns the focus of attention to those who have
remained in the community. "What you heard from the beginning" recalls the central revelation of God in the person of
Jesus which found expression in the confession that Jesus
was the Christ, the Son of God. Because those who remained
with the elder had confessed Jesus upon entering the community and maintained that confession in their corporate

worship, they have only to let that confession abide in them. The active agent here is the revelation of God within them; they had only to let it remain within them.

If we assume that the opponents had started with the same confession and later departed from it for one they found more adequate, these verses raise questions for all who experience faith as a growing, maturing experience. How can one advance through stages of faith without abandoning essential elements of that faith? Is faith a body of doctrine to be received and defended or an experience which must either deepen or die? Many (if not all) Christians begin with only a partial grasp of the Christian faith and find that they must grow, changing, revising, or discarding provincial or adolescent understandings. How then can one stay in touch with his or her religious beginnings? How can we let what we heard from the beginning abide in us without being bound to it? The opponents may well have charged that the elder and his group were bound by partial, elementary understandings; the elder charges that they have abandoned their faith in Jesus as the Christ.

On the other hand, the elder asserts, if the faithful will abide in the revelation they had received and the confession which marked their entrance into the community, they will have the continuing experience of abiding in the Son and the Father. The truth embodied in the essential belief and doctrine of the church could not change; their experience of it would endure, deepen, and mature. Through faith they would endure in that sphere of existence which belongs to God and is characterized by fellowship with him.

The experience of abiding is part of the greater reality of eternal life which is promised to all believers (John 3:16; 17:3). That promise of God was received through Jesus so it is difficult to decide who is meant by *he* in vs. 25. *Eternal life* for the Johannine community was a reality already present, which would continue beyond time (see 5:11–12). Through faith they had already "crossed over from death into life" (3:14), and fellowship with God through an enduring faith in Jesus Christ is itself the essence of that life.

The Christian's Anointing (2:26–27)

The elder's foremost concern is voiced in his brief description of the opponents. Because the elder seems to be referring to what he has been writing in 1 John, i.e., "these things," the verb may be translated either "I am writing" or "I have been writing." The veiled allusions of the preceding verses have been to the opponents, whom he now characterizes as "those who deceive [or mislead] you" (see 3:7). In the Gospel of John, Jesus is accused of leading the crowd into error (7:12), and those who marvel at Jesus are accused of having been deceived (7:47). Those who deceive the Johannine Christians are directed by the Spirit of Deceit which is opposed to the Spirit of Truth (4:6).

Quite naturally the elder returns to the anointing which the Johannine Christians had received, the anointing of the Spirit (see the discussion of this anointing above, 2:20). The Gospel of John records the promise of the Paraclete which would abide with the believers forever (John 14:16–17), remind them of all that Jesus had taught, and teach them all things (John 14:26). The Gospel recognizes both the need for later believers to be called back to the gospel tradition and the importance of the Spirit's function in leading them on to new perceptions and formulations of the truth: "I have yet many things to say to you ..." (John 16:12). The tension, again, is between the conservative principle and the liberal, the need to preserve and the need to adapt, the necessity of having roots and the necessity of being relevant. Both are important to the church. The elder emphasized the former, while his opponents apparently called for the latter.

In response to the specific danger that Johannine Christians might be misled by the opponents' teachings, the elder contends that Christians need no one to teach them because the Spirit teaches all things. The Spirit's teaching, moreover, is true. The last line of vs. 27 is ambiguous. It may be read either as a statement, "you abide," or as an imperative, "abide." Although one part of the Spirit's teaching is certainly that believers abide in Christ, an imperative element is clearly intended. The Johannine Christians must continue to abide and not be deceived. The abiding of which the elder writes may be either "in it" (the anointing, the teaching, or the Spirit) or "in him" (Christ). The latter is probably preferable, though it is a small point. The overriding issue is how to reconcile the elder's dismissal of the role of teachers with the importance accorded to them elsewhere in the NT (1 Cor 12:28–29; Eph 4:11; 2 Tim 1:11; Heb 5:12; James 3:1). Because of the common anointing of all Christians with the Spirit, the Johannine community apparently did not have official teachers or invest specific members with such authority. The elder himself does not claim authority over the community; instead he appeals to the authority of the community's tradition and his standing among the "we" which may designate the Johannine school, those who surrounded the Beloved Disciple. All members of the community were taught by God (John 6:45), so one did not need to teach another, which was also another aspect of the new covenant (Jer 31:34).

The difficulties of such an idealistic view of the church are readily apparent. Others would make the point that appointed teachers fulfill an important function, while the Spirit helps one to recognize the truth. The elder's point is an important part of the NT witness, even if it must be moderated by recognition of the specific threat which provoked his assertion, the limitations of the polity of the Johannine church, and the importance of other voices within the NT. Apart from the inner guidance of the Spirit, one may never find the truth among the competing voices of human teachers. The guidance of the Spirit may in fact be the only hope for those believers who are in danger of deception, or for the church in danger of schism.

This section moves from "The Hour of the Antichrists" (2:18) and "The First Schism" (2:19–21) to "The Christian's Confession" (2:22–25) and "the Christian's Anointing" (2:26–27). Do not be afraid of the biblical language. These units can provide the texts for a series of related sermons: "Antichrists in the American Church" (e.g., militarism, cultural idolatry, racial exclusivism, materialism), and "The Church: United and Divided," which may help Christians understand denominational distinctives yet value Christian unity. "The Christian's Confession" may suggest either of the following themes: "What It Means to Confess Christ" or "When Confession Brings Freedom." "The Christian's Anointing" is a particularly important topic because it will put believers in touch with the inner resources provided by the Holy Spirit while insuring that they do not fall prey to a false sense of self-sufficiency or independence from the Christian fellowship.

The Revelation of God's Children
(1 John 2:28—3:10)

This section is dynamically linked with the preceding sections. It extends the discussion of the division of light and darkness (2:9–11), the separation of the community from the world (2:12–17), and the opposition between the community and those who had departed from it (2:18–27). That separation now leads to a clear distinction between "the children of God" and "the children of the devil."

These expressions are drawn from traditional Johannine material, but they are here redefined to interpret for the community the danger it faces from its opponents. The prologue of the Gospel of John hinges on the term *the children of God*, which designates the new status of those who receive Jesus and believe. The Gospel then unfolds the significance of this new standing. Only those who follow Jesus—in contrast to the Jews—can truly understand the Scriptures and the heritage of Israel and live the life of the new era. They are born from above (John 3:3), drink living water (John 4), eat the bread of life (John 6), walk in the light (John 8—9), and have the resurrection and eternal life (John 11). They are the real brothers of Jesus (John 20:17–18).

The Gospel of John also lays down the theme which the elder will develop in these verses: the children of God share the nature of their Father. In the eighth chapter of John there is a sharp exchange between Jesus and the Jews. If a trial motif permeates the gospel, John 8 is a paternity suit. Who has the privilege of calling God their Father? The Jews claim Abraham and God as their fathers (John 8:39–41). Jesus responds that God cannot be their father because they do not do as God does; they do not love him, they do not hear his words. On the other hand, they are like their father, the devil, a liar and a murderer (John 8:44). At the base of this exchange is the principle that the children must be like their father. The elder now adapts that principle to the situation of the Johannine community in his time. In the process he places the Christian life in a new perspective for all future generations.

The internal structure of this passage is again open to debate. The introduction (2:28–29) is marked by a fresh address to the readers, "And now, little children. . . ." The last two verses (3:9–10) form a frame for the section and state its theme: the children of God and the children of the devil manifest their natures by what they do. The father's seed abides in the child. Raymond Brown treats 3:1–3 as an "exclamatory interruption." The remaining verses can then be divided into two strophes (2:28–29 with 3:4–6, and 3:7–10). The eight occurrences of the construction "everyone who" in 2:28–29 and 3:4–10 then provide the internal structure for each strophe. Edward Malatesta begins the section with 2:29, with 2:29—3:2 serving as the introduction and 3:9–10 as the conclusion. The body (3:3–8) he divides into three parts, which begin with 3:3, 6, and 7b.

Peter Rhea Jones (*Review and Expositor*, Fall 1970) uses the epistle's declarations of the attributes of God as clues to its major divisions: God is light (1:5—2:27), God is righteousness (2:28—4:6), and God is love (4:7—5:12). The preacher may find it helpful to pick up on the attributes and gifts of God which control this section: he is righteous (2:29; 3:7), he gives love (3:1) and hope (3:3), and he is pure (3:3). The children of God are therefore distinguished by their righteousness, love, hope, and purity.

The Confidence of the Righteous (2:28–29)

Verses 28 and 29 develop the theme of confidence at Christ's coming. In view of the continual interest of a large part of American Christianity in the "second coming," this section (2:28—3:10) offers the preacher a chance to channel that interest away from idle speculation and toward the task of developing essential Christian virtues.

The opening words of vs. 28, *and now,* pick up from the announcement of the arrival of the last hour in vs. 18. The readers, members of the Johannine community, have already been called *children* (2:1, 12, 14, and 18), though a different word is used in vs. 18. It is the elder's characteristic address to his readers (see 3:7, 18; 4:4; 5:21). Here the term is particularly apt since it introduces a section con-

cerned with the nature and qualities of Christians as the
children of God.

The phrase "abide in him" presents the same ambiguities
in vs. 28 as it did at the end of vs. 27. Context suggests that it
be interpreted as an imperative and that the pronoun refers
to Christ. The last hour is marked by the appearance of antichrists (2:18), so the coming of Christ can also be expected.
Abiding in him offers the believers a relationship in which
there can be no fear of condemnation (4:17). Abide in him,
therefore, the elder admonishes the community, "so that
when he appears we may have confidence." Abiding in
Christ, knowing him and experiencing his love now, is the
Christian's basis for confidence in the future. There is no uncertainty about Christ's coming. Although *ean* normally
means "if," it can also mean "when." The elder's point,
moreover, rules out any uncertainty; the Christian's present
experience allows the Christian to stand before the Lord confident of his righteousness. The use of "be shamed" in connection with Christ's parousia is reminiscent of the synoptic
saying, "For whoever is ashamed of me and of my words in
this adulterous and sinful generation, of him will the Son of
man also be ashamed, when he comes in the glory of his Father with the holy angels" (Mark 8:38; Luke 9:26, RSV). These
terms occur only here in the Johannine writings, but this
verse shows that apocalyptic expectation of Christ's coming,
though secondary, was not foreign to Johannine Christianity.

Verse 29 introduces the divine attribute which will domi-
nate the rest of this section: God is righteous (see 1:9; 2:1;
3:7). After 3:10 it occurs only once, however (3:12). *Righteousness* is not a dominant Johannine term, but the Gospel does
affirm that Jesus' judgment is righteous (John 5:30; 7:24) and
that the Father is righteous (John 17:25). The first occurrence
of the phrase "everyone who does" establishes the logic of
the rest of this section. The child is like the Father. If the
Father is righteous, then it stands to reason that everyone
who practices righteousness is born of God. *Righteousness* is
nothing less than the working out of God's justice; it involves
all that God does in establishing his sovereign will. To "do
righteousness," therefore, means to practice it as that pattern of life which comes from one's very nature. One who is
born of God can do nothing else, and nothing less. The elder's

opponents probably claimed to have been born of God also. The elder is preparing to charge, however, that they do not "do righteousness" and therefore cannot be children of God. The question to be raised in every new context should be, what does righteousness require of us? What will serve the end of establishing God's redemptive justice? The trailing edge of this verse demands that those who have no interest in establishing justice for others can hardly claim to be righteous. They are not God's children.

The Hope of the Righteous (3:1–3)

This paragraph is a joyful exclamation of the privileged status of the children of God. The previous verse ended with the assertion that the righteous have been born of God, but outsiders did not recognize them and those who had left the community may have claimed that they were children of God also. The elder therefore reassures the faithful of their standing and reminds them of the hope they share.

The first evidence that God regards them as his children is the love he has already given them. It is almost tangible. See how great and wonderful it is! Ours is a giving God. Quite a list of his gifts can be compiled from the Fourth Gospel: his Son (3:16), the Spirit (14:16), power to become children of God (1:12), living water (4:14), the bread of life (6:32), eternal life (10:28), peace (14:27), his word (17:14), his name (17:11–12), and whatever is asked in Jesus' name (15:16; 16:23). The Father's love was revealed in Jesus. Those who receive Jesus as the Son of God follow the new command, to love as he loved, and may therefore be called *children of God*. This designation is drawn from the covenant language of the OT (Hos 1:10; 11:1). The Sermon on the Mount also associates love and sonship: the peacemakers (Matt 5:9) and those who love their enemies (Matt 5:45) shall be called sons of God. This is the only place in the Gospel and Epistles of John where "calling" may have theological significance. It promises public and eschatological fulfillment of what is already a reality.

The believers are already children of God even if the world does not recognize them as such. In fact, rejection by the world is further confirmation of their status, since the world did not know their Lord either (see John 1:10; 8:19; 16:3;

17:25). The world, on the other hand, responded affirmatively to those who left the community, confirming thereby that they belonged to the world (4:5).

The Father's love has just been mentioned (3:1), so the common address to the community as "beloved" is all the more appropriate (see 2:7; 3:21; 4:1, 7, 11). The term names a community in which God's love is a reality. The words *now* and *not yet* show that God's work is not complete. We are already his children, and that will not change, but *"what* we shall be" has not been revealed. The confidence of those who have known God and abide in Christ is that when he appears they shall see that they are like him. Likeness to himself was the Creator's intention for his resistant creation, and his purpose shall yet be realized.

Our likeness to God shall be demonstrated because we shall see him. The Gospel of John proclaims the uniqueness of Jesus by denying that anyone else has seen God (1:18; 5:37; 6:46). On the other hand, all who had seen Jesus had seen the Father (John 14:9). Seeing God, with the knowledge of God and intimacy with him which it implies, is the ultimate hope of human existence (Rev 22:4). It is that which gives the promise of eternal life its value. We shall know as we are known when we see not in a mirror but face to face (1 Cor 13:12). But only the pure in heart shall see God (Matt 5:8); it is therefore a promise which belongs exclusively to the righteous (see Pss 11:7; 17:15).

Hope is an unstable compound, a precise blend of certainty and optimism. Put in too much assurance and certainty robs hope of its courage; put in too much optimism and hope turns pollyanna. The elder voices the biblical concept of hope, however. The Christian's hope is based on the character of God, his faithfulness, and his redemptive activity in the past. Faith nourishes the tender leaves of hope, but faith also requires obedience. All who have this hope purify themselves so that their hope may be fulfilled. For the elder, drawing on the language of the Gospel and the ritual of initiation into the community, purification meant being made clean and holy (see 1 Peter 1:22–23). Believers are made clean by his word and are sanctified in truth (John 13:10; 15:3; 17:19). If entrance into the community involved baptism and acclamation as children of God, then the elder is here reminding the faithful that continued purification is required of all who abide in Christ and hold the hope of seeing God. Those who hope for heavenly rewards but do not pursue righteousness have pipe dreams, not hope.

The Mission of the Righteous (3:4–6)

In the introductory verses of this section, the elder wrote of "everyone who does righteousness" (2:29). Now the corresponding opposite is named: "everyone who does sin" (3:4). The true gravity of all sin is exposed by the claim that sin is iniquity and one who lives sinfully lives in iniquity. *Iniquity* (Greek, *anomia*) here means more than "lawlessness." The word is used in significant contexts elsewhere in the NT to characterize the activity of the unredeemed, the wicked, and those in league with Satan (Matt 7:23; 13:41; 24:12; Rom 6:19; 2 Thess 2:3, 7; Titus 2:14). 2 Cor 6:14 opposed iniquity to righteousness in much the same way as the present context: "For what partnership have righteousness and iniquity?" Iniquity is characteristic of the antichrists mentioned earlier (2:18–19). The implication is that those who practice sin are certainly not born of God. The true nature of sin is that it exposes the inner nature of those it claims.

In the Gospel of John the presiding sin is unbelief (John 16:9), and Jesus came to take away sin (John 1:29). The elder here calls these passages in the Gospel, or common community tradition, to the minds of his readers by writing "and you know that." He uses *sin* in the plural, however, suggesting that not unbelief but recurring iniquity, violation of the covenant, and disobedience of the love command are in view. Earlier the elder emphasized the role of Jesus' death in "cleansing us from all sin" (1:7). He is our expiation (2:2). By characterizing the purpose of Jesus' manifestation in this way, the elder may be taking another swipe at the opponents' Christology, assuming that they emphasized revelation at the expense of the atoning significance of Jesus' death. The last element of vs. 5 affirms Jesus' sinlessness (John 7:18; Heb 4:15; 1 Peter 2:22), a claim the opponents would hardly have disputed. The problem was that they claimed to be sinless themselves (1:8, 10), while failing to show evidence of righteousness in their conduct.

Verse 6 draws the conclusion toward which this paragraph

has been building. If Christ came to remove sin and was sinless himself, then those who have been born of God and abide in Christ cannot continue in sin. Sin and righteousness are incompatible. Everyone who sins, therefore, has not seen him (see John 14:9) or known him. They do not and never could have belonged to the community of God's children. Their sin shows that they have no real knowledge of God. The question raised by this verse, which must be dealt with in the discussion of 3:9, is what the elder regards as sin. It is clear, however, from the earlier demand that sin be confessed (see the discussion of 1:9) that the elder recognized sin as a continuing reality in the life of the Christian. His point here is that Christ came to remove sin; the mission of the righteous can be no less, and must begin with the removal of sin from their own lives.

Children of a Righteous God (3:7–10)

The confidence, hope, and mission of the community all rest upon the members' relationship to God. If they are not his children, then all the rest crumbles. The repetition of the address with which this section began ("little children") signals the beginning of a new unit. The elder is moving to gather up the various lines of thought which have been developed from 2:28 on. His primary concern for the community is voiced in the exhortation, "let no one deceive you." We can only guess at the form of deception with which he is most concerned at this point. His thought has moved from correcting the Christology of the opponents to the status of the faithful as children of God (3:1–2, 10), the need for righteousness (2:29; 3:3, 7), and their freedom from sin (3:4–6, 8–9). Were the defectors charging that because the elder and his adherents continued to confess sin they were not righteous and were not free from sin? Or were they claiming that their freedom from sin rendered their manner of life a matter of no importance? Whatever the elder feared, he probably viewed their teachings as all the more dangerous because they were half-truths, perversions of the truth—but therefore not truth at all. His admonition recalls 1:8 and 2:26. The defectors deceive themselves, and he is writing to warn the community about their errors.

This section has focused on the righteousness of God (2:29), which must therefore also characterize the lives of his children. "Doing righteousness" (2:29; 3:7) is set in contrast to "doing sin" (3:4, 8). This way of putting it, using the present participle with a noun, not only emphasizes the contrast so that there are no other alternatives, but also depicts each alternative as a way of life. He does not mean "one who does a righteous deed" or "one who commits a sin." He is defining righteousness and sin as diametrically opposed and mutually exclusive ways of life, each sustained by a higher power. Righteousness presumably consists in keeping Jesus' commands (2:3), especially the new command (2:7–11; 3:10), and abiding in him (2:28) and in the tradition they had received from the beginning (2:27). Those who "do righteousness," so defined, show that they have been born of God (2:29) and are therefore righteous just as "that one" (apparently Christ, 3:3b, 5) is righteous.

Rather than returning to the link between sin and iniquity, the elder plays his ace. Those who live a life of sin are "from the devil" (3:8). They belong to the devil body and soul, but he does not say that they have been "born from him." The world is under his power (John 12:31; 14:30; 16:11), so a new birth is required only for those who become children of God. By the first century the devil had been identified with the serpent which tempted Eve, and blamed for Cain's murder of his brother (John 8:44; 1 John 3:12). All sin was therefore the work of the devil.

The phrase *for this* points ahead and will be explained by the purpose clause ("in order that") at the end of the verse (vs. 8). Following the theme of revelation, which is concentrated in this section (2:28; 3:2, 5, 8; but see earlier 1:2; 2:19), the purpose of Jesus' appearance is declared. In this context the incarnation was not primarily to reveal the Father and take away sin, as it is in the Gospel, but to destroy "the works of the devil." This phrase does not occur elsewhere in the NT, though the Gospel speaks of "the works of your father" (John 8:41) when "your father" means the devil. One does find the phrase "the work(s) of God" (6:28, 29; 9:3) and *work(s)* used to describe the fulfillment of God's redemptive activity in Jesus' ministry. For John, however, the destruction of the devil's work comes not by exorcisms, as in the Synoptic Gospels, but by Jesus' revelation of the Father, and that supremely in his death and exaltation.

1 John 3:9 is perhaps the most problematic verse in these epistles. First, there is the difficulty of being sure what it says: what is "his seed," and to whom do the two pronouns *his* and *him* refer? Second, how are this verse and the similar statements in 3:6 and 5:18 related to the apparently contradictory statements in 1:8 and 10? Finally, in what sense can this statement of the Christian's freedom from sin be true when the universal experience of the church is that sin continues to be a problem for believers?

The first part of vs. 9 is clear enough: "Everyone who has been born of God does not sin" (lit. "does not do sin," continuing the idiom of 3:4 and 3:8). The second part of the verse is subject to different interpretations, as the marginal notes in modern translations indicate.

1. "the offspring of God abide(s) in him," which may be interpreted in two ways:

a. taking *his seed*, here translated "the offspring of God," as Christ and *him* as the believer (JB)

b. taking *his seed* as the children of God and *him* as Christ or God (Moffatt, Perkins, RSV margin)

2. "God's seed abides in him," taking *him* as the believer; *his seed* may then refer to

a. God's nature (RSV, TEV)

b. God's word (de la Potterie, Dodd, Grayston, Malatesta)

c. the Holy Spirit (Brooke, Schnackenburg)

d. both God's word and the Holy Spirit (Marshall)

The first division takes *seed* (Greek, *sperma*) as meaning "offspring" or "descendant," as it does in John 7:42; 8:33, 37. Against this interpretation one must recognize that in all the Johannine references to Jesus as the Son of God and the believers as children of God, this idiom is not used. *His seed* is more often taken as an anthropomorphic reference to male seed. The RSV translation, "God's nature," introduces a term more suitable to the theories of patristic and medieval theologians. Although the interpretation of *his seed* as God's word has a venerable pedigree (Raymond Brown lists Augustine, Luther, Dodd, de la Potterie, Barclay, and others), taking the phrase as a reference to the Spirit is more defensible within the context of Johannine thought and within the argument of 1 John. The believer must be born of the Spirit (John 3:5) and have the Paraclete. The anointing mentioned in 2:20, 27 may also be a reference to the Spirit, and the Spirit figures prominently in the argument from this point on (3:24; 4:2, 6, 13; 5:6, 8). Because of the importance of the new covenant in 1 John, the promise in Ezek 36:26–27 may also be relevant: "and I will put my spirit within you." These considerations favor understanding 3:9 as claiming that those who have been born of God cannot sin because they have the Holy Spirit abiding in them.

Commentators have spared no ingenuity in attempting to resolve the tension between those passages in 1 John which recognize the reality of sin in the life of the Christian (1:8, 10) and those which claim there can be no sin in a Christian's life (3:6, 9; 5:18). Solutions which postulate multiple authors, editors, sources, or opponents do not solve the problem of how the finished product was meant to be understood. Moreover, it is doubtful that the difference in verb tenses (perfect in 1:10, aorist in 2:1, and present in 3:6, 9; 5:18—but present also in 1:8) can be made to resolve the difficulty. The present tense often suggests continued action, so it has been suggested that the verses may be harmonized by a strict interpretation of their grammar: believers cannot *continue to* sin but must recognize that they do sin. At a minimum, however, the author would have to be charged with depending too heavily on a subtle difference in grammar to make such a significant distinction.

At issue again is probably a difference between the elder and those who have left the community. Because both share the heritage of the Johannine tradition, with its sharp dualism and its perception of sin as arising from unbelief, both also hold to the view that those who have been born of God no longer belong to this world and are no longer under the power of evil. As God's children they have been delivered from sin. The elder recognizes both the continuing presence of sin in the lives of believers and the danger of assuming that the believer no longer needs to be concerned about sin. The opponents, however, may have exaggerated and distorted the community's emphasis on realized eschatology by claiming that believers were already free from sin. According to the Gospel, the ruler of this world has been cast out (John 12:31), but Satan can still enter a disciple (John 13:27). Therefore, the elder maintained that even the faithful must still confess their sin (1 John 1:8, 10). The ultimate deception is believing that one is incapable of deception. On the other hand, those who abide in Christ and have the Spirit abiding in them will lead lives characterized by righteousness rather than sin.

The lore of the Southern Baptist Theological Seminary preserves a story about one of its patriarchs, John R. Sampey, a true son of the Confederacy. Following the pedagogy of the day, Sampey quizzed one of his theology students:

"Could God sin?"

"No, sir," answered the student.

"Can you and I sin?"

"Yes, sir."

"Could Robert E. Lee sin?"

Uneasy, the student responded, "Yes, sir."

"No, sir; no, sir!" roared Sampey. "It was against his nature."

If Lee had been a member of his community, the elder would have agreed.

Verse 10 draws the logical conclusions, mincing no words. By their relationship to sin, both the children of God and the children of the devil (see John 8:44) are revealed. The elder has thus redefined and redirected the language of the Gospel (see John 8:44). Those who threaten the community are the children of the devil. In contrast, righteousness, as defined above (see the discussion of 2:29 and 3:7), characterizes the children of God; but there is another criterion as well, one that has already been introduced but which will be the theme of the last part of the epistle: love for one's brother.

Although this material is closely tied to the particular situation of the Johannine community, it stakes out truths which are relevant to the conflicts and struggles of every Christian community. We live between what is already fulfilled and what is not yet. The struggle with sin continues, but sin can be neither tolerated nor dismissed. Our relationship to God demands that we strive for perfection—for a life so characterized by righteousness and love that the inward reality of Christ's abiding presence is outwardly revealed. Christians, after all, are children of a righteous God.

If God is in any sense our Father, it means that we have an identity and a purpose that will transform the way we live. The preacher will find here a natural sequence of related themes: "Reclaiming Righteousness" (the virtue which is rooted in God's justice); "The Confidence of the Righteous" (knowing God as Father); "The Hope of the Righteous" (God's faithfulness, the fulfillment of God's work, face-to-face with God); and "The Mission of the Righteous" (eradicating sin, establishing justice, providing hope). The unifying theme "Children of a Righteous God" plays off of the title of the Broadway production "Children of a Lesser God."

Brotherly Love: The Command of the Covenant
(1 John 3:11–24)

Characteristically, the last verse of the preceding section was a transitional verse, reintroducing the new command that the children of God be marked by love for one another. Verse 11 begins a new section, and perhaps the second half of the epistle. The new beginning is signaled by the repetition of the declaration "This is the message which you have heard," which with minor variation ("we have heard") marked the beginning of the first section of the body of the epistle (1:5). The formula occurs nowhere else in the epistle. Internally, this section can be divided into an introduction (vss. 11–12), two parts (with vs. 18 forming either the conclusion of the first or the beginning of the second part), and a conclusion (vss. 23–24). The first part (vss. 13–18) interprets the specific requirements of the love command. Verse 18 is a transitional exhortation which begins with a fresh address to the community, "little children," similar to those which introduced earlier sections (2:1, 12, 18, 28; 3:7). It introduces the second part of this section with a reference to "truth." The second part (vss. 19–22) gives assurance that those who live by God's commands do not need to fear his judgment. The conclusion forms a frame for the section by repeating a variation of the opening line, "And this is his command," which is followed by a compound "that" (Greek, *hina*) clause which repeats the command to love one another.

The Community's Message: Love (3:11–12)

This section rides on the conclusion of the previous one. One who does not love his brother is not from God (vs. 10) because the definitive command which the community had received from the Beloved Disciple was that they should love one another (John 13:34). That is the message of the gospel, which they had both received from Jesus and had heard from the earliest days of the community. Its expression here echoes John 15:12 and resumes the elder's exposition of its re-

quirements, which began with 2:7–11. As has often been
noted, the Johannine love command is more limited than the
commands to love elsewhere in the NT (contrast Matt 5:44,
46; Luke 6:27, 32; 10:25–37). For the elder, however, love for
his enemies would have constituted love for the world (2:15)
since the opponents belonged to the world (4:5). On the positive side, there is a place for emphasis on the importance of
exemplary love within the Christian community (as in 1
Peter 1:22). Love for fellow Christians should be the purest
expression of that quality of character and life which God
desires for all.

To set off that love as sharply as possible, the elder appeals
to its archetypal antithesis: Cain, who murdered his brother.
The language of analogy ("just as"; Gk. *kathos*) is used frequently in 1 John to appeal to the authority of Jesus' life and
character (2:6; 3:3, 7; 4:17), Jesus' command (3:23), community tradition ("what you have heard," 2:18), or what they had
been taught (2:27). The phrase "not as" (*ou kathos*) occurs
only three other places in the NT (John 6:58; 14:27; 2 Cor
8:5).

Here Cain is said to be "from the evil one." The elder says
that Cain *slew* his brother, and the murder is traced to the
fact that "his works" were *evil* while his brother's were *righteous*. The language is carefully chosen to reflect graphically
the opposition between the community and those who had
left it. The "evil one" (surely synonymous with the devil; 3:8,
10) has been overcome (2:13, 14), so the faithful are secure
(5:18), but the world lies under his control (5:19). The term
slay is used elsewhere in the NT only in Revelation, where it
occurs eight times—for murder, martyrdom, and sacrificial
killings. Picking up the Lord's response to Cain, "If you do
well, will you not be accepted?" (Gen 4:7), the elder draws
the inference that Cain's offering was rejected because his
works were evil and his brother's was accepted because his
works were righteous. Both adjectives are significant. Evil is
the antithesis of righteousness (2:29), just as the evil one is
opposed to God. Evil marks all the works of those under the
power of the devil, including the antichrists who had gone
out from the community, just as righteousness marks the
children of God. In the Synoptic Gospels Jesus says that one
who is angry with his brother has committed murder (Matt

5:21–22), and the Gospel of John characterizes the devil as a murderer from the beginning (8:44). The elder's point is graphic: those who "hate" their fellow Christians are following the path of their "elder brother," Cain. Pointing to the end of a pattern of action may be the best way to prevent it, but the elder's spirit is less magnamious. He was not trying to reconcile the differences between himself and his opponents; his aim was to prevent further erosion of the community by exposing the defectors' actions as those of the devil.

Love in Community Life (3:13–18)

The change of address from "little children" to "brothers" is appropriate following the reference to Cain and his brother. In a community where love is expected, hostility may come as a surprise. Following the pattern of the Gospel's farewell discourse, where a warning concerning persecution follows the command to love, the elder reminds the community that hatred from the world is to be expected. This is the only verse in which 1 John connects hatred with the world, but the Gospel speaks of hatred as the world's response to Jesus' disciples (John 7:7; 15:18, 19; 17:14). The elder, on the contrary, repeatedly exposes the consequences of hating one's brother (2:9, 11; 3:15; 4:20). The world does not hate its own (John 7:7; 1 John 4:5), just as the children of God must love one another; but the world hates the brothers (3:13), and they must not love the world (2:15). Such are the relationships demanded by a rigid dualism which assumes that good and evil can be clearly and neatly distinguished.

Brotherly love is evidence of eternal life because it is the human experience which is most akin to the divine quality of that life. Regardless of the world's hostility, those who belong to the community know that they "have crossed from death into life" (3:14; see John 5:24; 13:1). In Johannine thought, Jesus himself is life (John 1:4; 14:6) and has the power to give life to those whom he loves (e.g., Lazarus); those who keep his word will never taste death (John 8:51–52). Eternal life has already begun for believers; its future aspect is merely the fulfillment of present reality. The reality of such life is expressed and demonstrated by the love one has for fellow believers. On the other hand, one who does not love—"his brother" is probably assumed, and some manuscripts supply these words—*remains* in death. Note that one does not cross over into death. There is no neutral ground. All are born blind, walk in darkness, and live in death unless they are born from above, receive their sight, cross from death into life, and abide in Christ. The surest sign of that life is the expression of God's love in love for one's brother or sister.

Everyone who does not love his brother hates his brother, and everyone who hates his brother is a murderer, like the devil (John 8:44; 1 John 3:8, 10) and like Cain (3:12). The elder has already charged that one who hates his brother is still in the darkness (2:9) and is blinded by it (2:11). If such a person says he loves God, he is a liar; he has not seen God and is not able to love (4:20).

The claim "and you know" (3:15b) builds on the previous claim "we know" in 3:14. "No murderer has eternal life abiding in him" is an axiom self-evident on several scores: murder was punishable by death (Gen 9:6; Exod 21:12), destruction of life is the work of the devil (John 8:44). If murder deprived one of the right to live, then would it not also deprive one of eternal life? For the elder, however, failure to love one's brother (i.e., *hate* and *murder*) shows that one does not have eternal life. Those who went out from the community did not cross over from life into death. They never had it; "they did not belong to us" (2:19). Those who have life abide in Christ, and those who come to him he will never cast out (John 6:37). The elder, therefore, seems not to allow that one could have eternal life and then lose it.

Verses 16–18 return to the meaning of the love command, which was introduced in vss. 11 and 14. Verse 16 states the general principle that we ought to love one another as Christ loved us, but it magnifies the principle by relating it to Christ's giving his life for his own. Verse 17 draws specific implications, and vs. 18 concludes the paragraph with an exhortation to show love through what one does, not just by what one says.

"In this we have come to know" (vs. 16), which is so characteristic of 1 John's idiom, points ahead to the clarifying "that" clause. Christ's death revealed the true nature and depth of God's love. If those who left the community made little of the significance of Christ's death in their doctrine of salvation, then the elder may be charging that they do not know what love is because they failed to see it in the death of Jesus. The expression "to lay down" one's life does not occur in the NT outside this verse and eight references in the Gospel of John (10:11, 15, 17, 18 [twice]; 13:37, 38; 15:13), where it is used both for Jesus' death and for Peter's death. If 3:11 echoes John 15:12, then 3:16 picks up the next verse: "No one has greater love than this: that he lays down his life for his friends" (John 15:13). Use of the word *psyche* rather than *zoe* for life in the Gospel of John is confined to the eight references listed above and the parallel references in John 12:24, 25, 27. It denotes natural, mortal life as opposed to eternal life. Christ did not give up his eternal life! With two exceptions (John 1:30; 11:4), all of the occurrences of the word *for* (*hyper*, "on behalf of") in the Gospel refer to Jesus' (or Peter's) death (in addition to the references listed above, see John 6:51; 11:50–52; 17:19; 18:14). The word is also used in the Synoptic Gospels in the words of institution at the Last Supper (Mark 14:24; Luke 22:19, 20). The language of 3:16, therefore, has deep roots in the interpretation of Jesus' death in the early church and the Johannine community in particular.

The second part of vs. 16 draws the ethical imperative: "so we ought to lay down our lives for the brothers." Following the references to *brothers* earlier in this section, the elder favors the term over the Gospel's statements that Jesus laid down his life for the life of the world (John 6:51), for his sheep (John 10:11, 15), for the people (John 11:50–52; 18:14), or for his friends (John 15:13). The "ought" of Christian living arises first and foremost from the example of Christ's life (John 13:14; 1 John 2:6; 4:11).

Talk about love comes easily in the Christian community, but what does the love command really mean? What is required by the command to "lay down our lives"? Verse 17 consists of a series of three conditions followed by a devastating question: "Whoever has ... and sees ... and closes ... how ...?" The elder returns to a word for life (*bios*) which he used earlier when describing the things of the world (2:16). He does not condemn having the means of life but warns the faithful against the pride, arrogance, and misplaced confidence which so often accompany possessing material goods. At least some of the faithful had "worldly goods." The elder probably had in mind both members of the community and those who had left it. In view of the fact that he has called the defectors "antichrists," it is difficult to think that he is here calling for the community to share their goods with those who had gone out from the community if the latter are in need. The elder never calls the defectors "brothers." On the other hand, he may be condemning the defectors for not sharing their goods with those among the faithful who are in need. If such is the case, it illustrates the blindness which often afflicts those caught up in schisms and controversies within the church. The force of this verse should not be limited to the wealthy only. *Need* and *abundance* are relative terms. *Agape* demands that those who are full give to those who are hungry, that those who "can't find anything to wear" give to those who would be glad to have something to wear (see Deut 15:7; James 2:15–16). If one has no compassion and shuts out a needy brother, how can "the love of God" remain in such a person? The phrase may refer either to our love for God or God's love for us. Later the elder will say that love comes from God (4:7). Here the point is that one shows that he has not been claimed by God's love if he does not show love for a brother in need. Ultimately, of course, the demand of love must break the limitation of community exclusiveness, but if it is not found within the community, how can the brotherhood of all be realized?

The concluding exhortation is appropriate. "Brothers," after all, are related because they are "children." The challenge is to show that the traditional words, dulled by repetition, represent a reality in one's life. The exhortation to be "doers of the word, and not hearers only" is common in the NT (James 1:22, RSV; Matt 7:24–27; 23:3; Luke 6:46–49; 11:28; 12:47; Rom 2:13). The elder is saying more, however. *Work* and *truth* are important terms for the Johannine writers. Jesus' works embraced all that he did which fulfilled his redemptive mission to do his Father's work. Moreover, the elder has already emphasized the importance of having the truth abiding in oneself and "doing the truth" (1:8, 10). Both of the shorter letters begin with the elder's assurance that he loves the recipients "in truth" (2 John 1; 3 John 1).

Truth, therefore, is the origin of love's work just as the
tongue is the source of one's words. It cannot be otherwise;
love allows no deceit or hypocrisy. Its counterfeit is not love
at all.

Assurances to Those Who Know God's Love
(3:19–22)

Verses 19–21 pose a baffling array of textual, grammatical, and exegetical problems. As Raymond Brown com-
ments, "the epistolary author is singularly inept in
constructing clear sentences, but in these verses he is at his
worst." Careful comparison of modern translations and
study of full-scale commentaries will be needed to reveal all
of the alternatives these verses afford translators and interpreters. One's conclusions, however, are likely to be guided
more by decisions regarding the context and theological
emphases of the epistle than by minute analysis of the manuscript and grammatical data.

Is the author responding to the nagging guilt of the faithful, who know they have not loved one another as they
ought? Or is he responding to the charges of the defectors,
who may have troubled members of the community by saying that they were not really righteous because they were
worried about sinning (see 1:8, 10)? More significant still, is
the elder assuring his readers that they can have confidence
before God even if they know they are not blameless (see
Brown)? Is he urging them to be sinless by warning that
God's judgment upon them will be even more severe than
their judgment on themselves (see Grayston)? Or is he saying that we can have confidence because God, who knows
all things, can be more objective (see Marshall)? The tone
seems to be one of assurance, and the elder has already in-
sisted that there is forgiveness for those who confessed their
sins. The reassuring interpretation is to be preferred, therefore, over the severe or mediating positions, as analysis of
the details of these verses shows.

The troublesome phrase "by this" here refers to what precedes it (vs. 18). Acts of love, which stem from the truth that
abides within us, show that we are "from the truth." Three
different idioms are used in vss. 19, 21, and 22, each of
which means "before him [God]"; there is no material dif-

ference in meaning. The elder is probably focusing on the
believer's present relationship to God, but he does not exclude fulfillment of the judgment in the future. The Gospel
of John emphasizes that the believer has already been delivered from judgment (3:19; 5:24), which may have given rise
to the opponents' claim that they were sinless. The elder,
therefore, revives the early Christian preaching of the
parousia (1 John 2:28—3:3; 4:17). The verb in 19b, *peitho*,
means "convince" but can mean "to reassure." It does not
occur elsewhere in the Johannine writings. Even if we, "our
hearts," are aware of our sinfulness and failure to fulfill the
love command, God is greater. The assurance, apparently,
is that God is more ready to forgive us than we are to accept
the fact that he has forgiven us. The elder's reminder that
God knows all things serves as contrast to the references in
vss. 20a and 21a to what our hearts "know against us." We
are children of no lesser God. Often those most conscious of
their sinfulness are those who are most surely forgiven. On
the other hand, if we are blameless, if our hearts do not
condemn us—a condition the elder recognized as not only
possible but desirable for believers—then we may have confidence before God (see 2:28).

The general confidence which the righteous can have
before God, now and in the future, is illustrated specifically
by the Johannine assurances regarding prayer. The Gospel
of John features several such promises:

> If you knew ... you would have asked him, and he would
> have given you living water (4:10).

> I know that whatever you ask from God, God will give you
> (11:22).

> Whatever you ask in my name, I will do it, ... if you ask
> anything in my name, I will do it. If you love me, you will
> keep my commandments (14:13-15).

> If you abide in me, and my words abide in you, ask what-
> ever you will, and it shall be done for you (15:7).

> ... so that whatever you ask the Father in my name, he may
> give it to you. This I command you, to love one another
> (15:16-17).

> If you ask anything of the Father, he will give it to you in my
> name. ... Ask, and you will receive (16:23-24, RSV).

Several of these passages are preceded or followed immediately by exhortations to keep his commands. The assurance of answered prayer in 1 John is not necessarily based on one's merit, however. Underlying much of the theology of the epistle is the application of the promises of the new covenant to the Johannine community. That covenant relationship cannot be presumed upon—as the elder may feel his opponents were doing by claiming that their actions no longer mattered (e.g., iniquity, 3:4; closing one's heart to a needy brother, 3:17). The covenant people will receive whatever they ask because they maintain their covenant relationship: they keep his commandments (see the discussion of 2:3–5) and do what is pleasing before him (3:22b; see John 8:29). The elder will return to this theme in 5:14–15, where prayer is again related to the confidence of the faithful.

These verses are likely to pose theological problems for many contemporary Christians. Is righteousness before God really possible? Are not promises of answered prayer hollow? Are they tied to such a high demand—keeping his commands—that we are incapable of attaining them? For just this reason, however, attention should be focused on this section of 1 John. God is greater than both our efforts to be righteous and our sensitive Western consciences, and his greatness is shown in his goodness toward us. Our righteousness, on the other hand, does not depend on our own efforts or on our feelings about ourselves. It comes from the Spirit which God has given us. Not surprisingly, the elder turns to the gift of the Spirit in the conclusion of this section (3:24) and in the next part of the letter (4:1–6).

The Twofold Command: Believe and Love
(3:23–24)

The conclusion to this section sums up the elder's understanding of what it means to be a Christian as well as any verse in the epistle. It is a definitive statement of "the message which you heard from the beginning" (3:11)—the words with which this section began. The command is twofold, and both parts are drawn from the Gospel: believe in the name of his Son, Jesus Christ (John 1:12; 3:16; 14:1; 20:31), and love one another (John 13:34; 15:12). This twofold command is the Johannine version of the great command to love God and love your neighbor as yourself (Mark 12:28–31; Deut 6:4; Lev 19:18). While the love command has already been treated extensively (2:7–11; 3:11, 16–18), this is the first reference to believing. The command to believe will recur throughout the rest of the letter, however. Here it is attached to "the name of his Son." Believing in Jesus (5:1, 5, 10), or in his name (5:13), is tantamount to receiving his revelation of the Father and the salvation he offers (John 3:18). It was also the requirement for membership in the Christian community and surely figured prominently in its worship, its instruction of new converts, and its practice of baptism.

These commands are the conditions of the covenant. Those who keep them (see 2:3) can be assured, therefore, that they abide in God and God abides in them. They have his words, his anointing, and can therefore share his fellowship and his eternal life. That assurance is sufficient to overcome either personal self-doubt or the accusation of outsiders, who in the context of 1 John may have charged that those faithful to the elder did not really abide in God because they were still concerned about their sinfulness. One's sense of guilt is overcome not by being unconcerned about righteousness nor by convincing oneself that one has done nothing wrong but by believing in Christ and by loving one's brother and sister. "In this we know" (vs. 24b) again points ahead. Ultimately it is the gift of his Spirit which confirms to us that we abide in God and that he has accepted us into his fellowship. It is also the gift of the Spirit (vs. 24b) which enables us to keep the commandment he has given (vs. 23b). God is the giver of both, and that is another measure of his greatness (3:20), another reason that his children can be confident before him. Sermons on this section should dramatize the distinctive character of Christian love. Love is demonstrated not by the way we feel toward persons in need but by what we do for them. Love for a brother leads to life; hate leads to death. This section can be related to the OT lesson (Gen 4:1–16) and to a Gospel text (Matt 5:21–24). Did Jesus have the story of Cain and Abel in mind when he said, "So if you are offering your gift at the altar, and there remember that your brother has something against you, leave your gift there before the altar and go; first be reconciled to your brother, and then come and offer your gift" (Matt 5:23–24, RSV)? The abandoned offering can be a sign that the church is about the work of reconciliation. Note the tension between the three texts: according to Genesis, God had no regard for Cain's offering (but instructed him to do good); according to 1 John, Cain's works were evil; according to Jesus, Abel should have left his offering and gone to be reconciled to Cain. A sermon title can be drawn from any of the three texts: Genesis: "Worshiping East of Eden," "Keeping Brothers Brothers"; Matthew: "Before You Seek God," "The Abandoned Offering"; 1 John: "How to Have God's Love" (3:17), "The Ultimate Choice" (to take life or lay down life, 3:15–16), "Love in Work and Truth" (3:18).

Two Spirits—Two Tests
(1 John 4:1–6)

The twin themes announced at the end of the last section—belief and love—are treated at length throughout 1 John 4. In the last line of chapter 3 a new term also appears for the first time in the epistle: *spirit.* Jesus had promised the coming of the Paraclete, the Holy Spirit (John 14:16–17), and very likely both the Johannine Christians and those who had gone out from them claimed that God had given them the Spirit. Prophets played a significant role in the life of the early church, speaking directly for God under the inspiration of the Spirit and providing direction for the church. Gradually a more official structure—bishops and deacons—replaced the earlier charismatic leadership of the church through apostles, prophets, and teachers. In part this change occurred because of the problem of false prophets. The Johannine community had not yet developed official leadership. The elder appeals to his authority as one who represented the tradition of the community, but he could not dictate what the community should do simply by virtue of his office.

Religious leaders, prophets, and charlatans have often claimed to be authorized by God's Spirit. Today, with a fragmented church, cults sprouting like weeds, and mass media broadcasting the voices of all who are powerful or persuasive enough to gain attention, the ability to "test the spirits" is essential. How then can the believing community distinguish among the many competing voices? Which speak with divine authority and which are wolves in sheep's clothing? That is the question to which 1 John 4:1–6 directs its readers. Preaching on this section will help those who are bewildered to have some "Tests for Faith."

Verse 1 appeals to the need to test the spirits because there are many false voices. Verses 2 and 3 state the first criterion: content. Those who confess Jesus Christ who has come in flesh are from God; those who do not are from the antichrist. Verse 4 assures the faithful that the Spirit of God in them is more powerful than the spirit at work in the world. Verses 5 and 6 state the second criterion: reception. Those who listen to the community belong to God; those who listen to its opponents belong to the world. There are two spirits, therefore: a spirit of truth and a spirit of deception.

Who Speaks the Truth? (4:1–3)

Beloved is chosen over *little children* or *brothers* as the term of address in this part of the letter (3:21; 4:1, 7, 11; see 2:7; 3:2). The command not to believe in every spirit but to test the spirits should be interpreted literally against the prevailing world view of the first century, according to which the world was populated by various kinds of angels, demons, and unclean spirits. The Qumran community taught that there were two spirits—a spirit of truth/light and a spirit of falsehood/darkness—and that both were present in differing degrees in each person (*Manual of Discipline* 3:13—4:26). How one lived revealed which spirit dominated one's life. When the elder writes "do not believe in every spirit," the implication is that there are various spirits or kinds of spirits. In contemporary terms we might say that just because someone claims to be directed by God or speaks or acts in ways commonly associated with inspiration is no guarantee that they are speaking the truth or doing what is right. The verb *to test* is drawn from the testing of coinage to distinguish those which are genuine from those which are counterfeit (see *Didache* 12:1, which also deals with false prophets). Unfortunately, there are influential counterfeits from whom the faithful need protection, because naive piety is often blinded by sparkle and oblivious to substance. Not all "spirits" are from God.

The verb *to go out* is used in 1 John only twice: once here and once to describe the "antichrists" who went out from the community (2:19; see 2 John 7). It seems justified, therefore, to assume that the elder has the same group in mind when he says, "Many false prophets have gone out into the world." Had they not been a part of the community at one time the elder would not have said that they "went out." In going out, however, they repeated the action of Judas, who went out into the darkness (John 13:30). By going out into the world, the defectors joined those forces which are opposed to the believing community and subjected themselves to the spirit at work in the world. They continued to claim faith in Christ and the gift of the Spirit teaching them all things (2:27). *False prophets* are those who claim to speak for God or claim to have his Spirit but deceive and mislead God's people. How then can they be exposed? Deut 13:1–5 imposed the criterion of content: even if the prophet's sign or wonder comes to pass, if he calls for worship of another god, do not listen to him.

The elder probably felt that he faced an analogous situation. The phrase "in this" points ahead to the second half of vs. 2; it is parallel to the "in this" in 3:24. The criterion given there is that only those who have the Spirit of God utter a true confession (see 1 Cor 12:3). It is difficult, however, to know exactly what constitutes a true confession or what separates it from the confession of the elder's opponents. Clearly, 1 John 4:2 adds a phrase to the confession toward which the Gospel of John leads its readers (John 20:31), but commentators have interpreted that phrase variously:

> "every spirit which confesses Jesus Christ come in the flesh" (Brooke, Brown, Grayston)

> "every spirit which confesses Jesus Christ as come [or "as having come"] in the flesh" (Bultmann, Marshall)

> "every spirit which confesses [or acknowledges] that Jesus Christ has come in the flesh" (KJV, RSV, NIV, NASB, NEB; Houlden, Malatesta; note: the word *that* is not in the Greek text)

> "every spirit which confesses Jesus as the Christ having come in flesh" (Dodd, Moffatt, Stott)

The first alternative is the most literal, but suffers from the same obscurity as the Greek text. Separating *Christ* from *Jesus*, as the last proposal does, is unwarranted in view of the common use of the title with the name, "Jesus Christ," in 1 John (1:3; 2:1; 3:23; 4:15; 5:6, 20). The only other occurrences of *Christ* are preceded by the article, "the Christ" (2:22; 5:1). The second and third possibilities are only slightly different and may be preferred for their clarity so long as one does not construe *Christ* as a title for the preexistent *logos*.

Beyond translation, one must ask why the confession was formulated in this way. If the required confession is a response to a confession the author deems false, what was that confession? Perkins denies that it can be reconstructed. Brown postulates that the opponents denied the significance of what Jesus was or did in the flesh. Bultmann and others argue that the opponents denied the reality of the incarnation; the Christ did not appear in the historical Jesus. Other statements of confession in 1 John may be of some help in interpreting the nuance of this compressed confession, which is no doubt meant to carry more meaning than it clearly expresses. The elder requires belief "that Jesus is the Christ" (5:1; see 3:23), and brands as a liar anyone who denies "that Jesus is the Christ" (2:22). Both the affirmation that Jesus was the Christ and the affirmation that the Christ came in flesh are essential. Holding either without the other not only is insufficient but exposes one as an antichrist and false prophet. The opponents affirmed the divinity of Jesus but denied or diminished the significance of his humanity, perhaps to protect the confession that he was divine. That tendency continues in modern Christianity, and is today probably the most prevalent heresy among committed Christians. Denying the divinity of Christ is the error of unbelievers; diminishing the significance of his humanity is the error of many well-meaning Christians. Neither the elder nor the Gospel writers saw any conflict in affirming both Jesus' humanity and his divinity, however. Affirming one does not require denying the other. Moreover, by neglecting the human side of Jesus one jeopardizes the importance of his identification with humanity, the significance of his sinlessness, and the reality of his suffering. In some form, that is probably what the elder feared his opponents had done.

Verse 3 again poses textual problems. The most significant are whether the main verb is "does not confess" or "annuls" (Greek, *luei*) and whether to make the verse parallel with the preceding one by adding the phrase "come in flesh." The latter seems clearly to be a scribal addition. Good arguments can be made for the reading "annuls" (e.g., Brown), but its manuscript support is very weak. The difference, anyhow, is not great. The effect of vs. 3, coming after the more specific confession in vs. 2, is to say that any person ("spirit") who

denies or diminishes the significance of Jesus' humanity does
not confess that Jesus was the incarnate Christ, and therefore
does not belong to God. In fact, that person belongs to the
antichrist. The elder again appeals to common early Christian tradition: the readers had all heard that the antichrist
would come before the end (2:18). The appearance now of
antichrists, those under the influence of the evil spirit opposed to Christ, who showed their allegiance by denying the
humanity of Jesus, was a sign that the endtime had come.
The fact that such apocalyptic evil makes its appearance in
every generation does not diminish its threat. Half-truths are
always more dangerous than clearly discernible falsehoods,
particularly when it comes to Christology and its implications for the Christian life.

Several sermon titles could be used for this section: "Exposing False Prophets," "When Half-Truths Are Entirely
False," or "Who Knows the Truth?"

Who Hears the Truth? (4:4–6)

The new paragraph begins with a personal address to the
faithful readers, "you," and assures them that they belong to
God. They have conquered the antichrists, the false prophets
who had gone out from the community into the world. *Conquer* is a word the elder uses with several related objects:
"the evil one" (2:13, 14), "them" (4:4), and "the world" (5:4,
5; see John 16:33). Those who conquer are the "young men,"
"you," those who have been born of God, and those who believe that Jesus is the Son of God. The language of victory
also plays a prominent role in the book of Revelation. The
victory is assured, even though those who went out from the
community may have been the more numerous, more pros-
perous, or more influential group. Perhaps contrary to appearances or the morale of the community, the faithful were
assured of victory because the spirit within them was
stronger than the spirit of the antichrist which was at work
in the world. By leaving the community, the false prophets
had gone out into the world and had come under the power
of the ruler of this world (John 12:31; 14:30; 16:11).

Verse 5 introduces the second criterion: reception. The
world receives those who belong to it, just as the children of
God receive his word. Because the defectors really belong to

the world, what they say comes from the world, the things of the world (2:15), and the spirit which controls the world. They are indeed inspired, but it is not the Spirit of God which is inspiring their speech. According to the Gospel of John, one can only speak what one hears, or what is given: "he who is of the earth belongs to the earth, and of the earth he speaks" (3:31); "he whom God has sent utters the words of God" (3:34, RSV; see 7:16–18, 46; 12:50; 14:10; 16:13). Because the false prophets speak falsely, they must be instructed by the Spirit of Deception. Similarly, because they are inspired by the world's spirit, the world responds to their message.

The same pattern of reception reveals those who belong to God. Because "we" belong to God, those who know God hear "us." Conversely, those who do not belong to God will not receive the words of those who are faithful to him. Their experience bore out the truth of their Gospel: "he calls his own sheep by name, . . . and the sheep follow him, for they know his voice" (John 10:3–4, RSV). This dualism of responses—the fact that some listen to the false prophets, while others hear the faithful—finally reveals that there are two spirits at work, not one. There is the Spirit of Truth, which dwells in the believers, and the Spirit of Deception, which inspires false prophets. The Spirit of Truth is another way in which the Johannine writers refer to the Holy Spirit or the Paraclete (John 14:17; 15:26; 16:13). Very likely the elder thought that he was being guided by the Paraclete, guiding the community into all truth (John 16:13) while convicting the world of sin (John 16:8–9). The Spirit of Deception is not mentioned elsewhere in the NT, but the elder has already warned the community against deception: "if we say we have no sin, we deceive ourselves" (1:8); "I have written these things to you concerning those who are deceiving you" (2:26); and again, "children, let no one deceive you" (3:7). Deception of the faithful is therefore unmasked as the work of the Spirit of Deception. It could also be tied to Satan, who entered Judas as Jesus was speaking of the Paraclete that would come to the disciples (John 13:27; 14:23, 26).

The full extent of the dualism of 1 John is now clear and may be sketched in the following diagram.

	God
the antichrist, the devil	Christ
the Spirit of Deception	the Spirit of Truth
the children of the devil	the children of God
the world	the Johannine community
antichrists, false prophets	the brothers, beloved
the defectors, who went out into the world	those faithful to the elder
they	we, you

There is no middle ground, no gray area, no room for compromise. Nevertheless, the dualism is not complete, as in some philosophical systems, because there is no cosmic counterpart to God. The devil is the antichrist of the last days, and he has already been conquered (2:13, 14). The devil is the liar (John 8:44), and he works through the Spirit of Deception (4:6). Those under his power may be called children of the devil (3:10). The world lies under his power (5:19), so the faithful cannot love the world or the things that belong to it (2:15–17). Those who went out from the community have come under the antichrist; they are antichrists, false prophets inspired by the Spirit of Deception. They deny that they have any sin, but tragically they have no escape from it. On the other hand, those who are faithful to the elder, the remnant of the Johannine community, are children of God, beloved brothers and sisters. Christ abides in them through the Spirit of Truth, because they confess Jesus Christ who came in flesh, and because of the abiding presence of the Spirit of Truth they know that they have the truth and belong to God. The logic is clear and irrefutable; but as we can see from 1 John itself, it was probably ineffective in dealing with the schism of the community. The other group probably had an equally clear defense and may have been just as exclusive in its relationship to the Johannine community.

The continuing significance of this section may be its clear-eyed recognition that there are people who claim inspiration but pose a serious threat to the church. Where there are conflicting voices within the church two tests may be applied: what are they saying, and who is listening to them? More specifically, are the religious leaders affirming the historic confessions of the church or are they advocating departures from the church's doctrines? Who is being influenced by them? Those who have provided leadership for the church over the years, or those whose commitment to the believing community has yet to be tested? While these tests may not be sufficient, they are at least in the spirit of those offered by 1 John 4:1–6 as a defense for the community.

The Perfect Love
(1 John 4:7–21)

The Johannine double command in 3:23 requires that we believe in the name of Jesus Christ and that we love one another. Keeping that command is possible because the one who gave the command also gave his Spirit. The previous verses (4:1–6) clarified the criteria by which his Spirit can be discerned, so the elder now returns to the new command of community love. This is the third, and most profound, treatment of love in 1 John. This section and 1 Cor 13 stand as the NT's most moving testimonies to the true nature of love. The simple language of both passages gives expression to truth that defies complicated explanation.

In 1 John 2:7–11 the command to love one's brother was introduced as a sign that one was living as Christ had lived (2:6), and therefore was walking in the light. Such community love demands that one not love the world which is opposed to God's children (2:15). The Father has given his children love (3:1), and this will be the theme of much of 4:7–21. The second section devoted to the theme of love (3:10–18) treats love for a brother as the epitome of righteousness. Love may require laying down one's life, as Christ did, or giving food or shelter to a brother in need (3:16–17). Major sections of 1 John are marked by "God is" statements: "God is light" (1:5), and "he is righteous" (2:29), and now "God is love" (4:8). It is significant, therefore, that love is treated in each part of 1 John. Having been related to light in 2:7–11, 15, and righteousness in 3:1, 10–18, its origin as the expression of God's character and its fulfillment in our own experience will now be unfolded. *Perfect love* (4:18) may be taken as a unifying homiletical theme for this section. Although there is no consensus as to the number or length of the units in this section, I have chosen to break it into three units: the source of perfect love (4:7–10), the experience of perfect love (4:11–16a), and the confidence of perfect love (4:16b–21). These divisions could serve as the outline for an expository sermon. The love command continues to occupy the elder's attention through 5:4 (see Brown), but 5:1–4 may also be regarded as the introduction to the next unit. It is characteristic of 1 John to have transitional verses which may be placed with either what precedes them or what follows them.

The Source of Perfect Love (4:7–10)

The opening word is doubly significant: it continues the form of address found in 3:21, 4:1, and 4:11; but more importantly it reminds us that those who are commanded to love others are themselves *beloved*. The words "let us love one another" recur like a refrain (3:11, 23; 4:7, 11, 12). The alternate version of the command, "love one's brother" (2:10; 3:10, 14; 4:20, 21; see 5:2), shows that the elder focused on the requirement that members of the Johannine community love one another. The remainder of vs. 7 and all of vs. 8 form an inclusion, such as may be found in many other verses in 1 John:

A		Love is from God
B		and everyone who loves
	C	has been born of God
	D	and knows God.
B'		He who does not love
	D'	does not know God
A'		because God is love.

The structure is not perfect—few are—but it clearly attributes love to God and establishes love as a criterion for distinguishing those who know God (and are his children) from those who do not. The criterion is stated in both a positive and a negative form. Earlier criteria have followed the theme of the section in which they appear. Because God is light his children must walk in the light (1:7), but that involves recognizing and confessing one's sinfulness (1:8, 10) and keeping God's commands (2:3), above all the command to love one another (2:7–11). Because God is righteous, everyone who practices righteousness has been born of him (2:29). Such righteousness involves both sinlessness and sacrificial love for one's fellow Christian (3:9–10).

The A and A' clauses in vss. 7–8 affirm that the source of perfect love is God himself because love is essential to the very character of God. He does not command his own to do anything but what they learn from fellowship with him (see John 5:19). When the elder asserts that everyone who loves has been born of God, he still focuses on the difference between faithful members of the Johannine community and those who oppose them. He certainly does not mean that whenever any person demonstrates love for another human being one can be assured that that person has been born of God. That may be true in some diminished, natural sense, in that God is the Creator of all and has left something of his character in every person; but the elder means that all who practice love for their fellow Christians within the church show thereby that they have come to know something of God's character and are living in response to him as his children.

Earlier it was said that those who have been born of God, i.e., the children of God, practice righteousness (2:29) and cannot sin (3:9). The meaning of being born of God will be explored further in the next chapter, but it is hardly surprising that birth from God is here tied to that quality which most distinguishes who God is and what he does: love. Knowledge of God is therefore manifested not in some esoteric lore, nor in the arrogance of the unenlightened (see 1 Cor 8:1–3), but in a quality of character and life that can come only from God. In the next several verses the elder will turn his attention to how it is possible for us to know God's love and participate in it. In vs. 8, however, his attention turns back to his opponents. Because they do not love the Johannine Christians, they show that they do not know God. The negation is forceful and may even be interpreted "they never knew God" or "they have not begun to know God."

There is no more simple, sufficient, or profound statement in the whole Bible than "God is love" (4:8). Every Sunday school child learns it, yet no theologian fully grasps its significance. Paul concluded 1 Cor 13 with the words, "So faith, hope, love abide, these three; but the greatest of these is love." Faith and hope will pass away when we know as we are known, but love endures because it alone is rooted in the character of God himself.

Verse 9 offers an explanation of how God's love was revealed. It is a summary of the gospel, John's Gospel in particular. 1 John began with affirmation that Life had been manifested to us in Jesus Christ (1:2). Jesus had revealed his glory (John 2:11), the works of God (John 3:21; 9:3), and the Father's name (John 17:6). He was manifested after his resurrection (John 21:1, 14), and he will be manifested at his coming (2:28; 3:2). He came to bring forgiveness for sin and destroy the works of the devil (3:8). In the epistle's last reference to *revelation*, the incarnation of Jesus is related to the revelation of God's love for us. *The love of God* here means "God's love"; *in us* may be taken to the most personal level, not just "for us" or "among us" but "within us," as 4:12 and 4:16b–17 indicate.

This revelation of God's love was achieved through the sending of his unique Son, through whom all who believe in him become children of God. Just as God loved the Son (John 3:35; 10:17; 15:9), so the Father and Son both love God's children and abide with them (John 14:21; 17:23–26). This verse echoes the familiar John 3:16. Compare the two closely: *God, loved, the world, sent, only Son, life.* These words are essential to any summary of the Johannine gospel. In contrast to the Gospel, 1 John does not say that God loved the world, however (see 2:15). Jesus came to make expiation for the sins of all the world (2:2), and he is the Savior of the world (4:14); but the world has not known him or received him. It preferred darkness rather than light, iniquity over righteousness, and hatred over love; but although it lies in the power of the evil one (4:4; 5:19), the world has been defeated and is passing away (2:17; 5:4–5). That is the terrible consequence of love rebuffed, forgiveness rejected. On the other hand, God sent his Son so that "we"—those who would believe in him— might have the life of eternity through him. That life, though it cannot be fully realized in the present, so transforms the lives of the faithful, opening for them the possibility of knowing God, living righteously, and loving one another, that the elder can say that they have "passed over from death into life" (3:14). God's love is therefore revealed *in us*, through the life that the incarnation of Jesus made possible.

Verse 10 extends the thought of vs. 9. Love is not realized by human effort but by divine disclosure. If we are able to love one another or love God, it is only because we have experienced his love for us. Forgiveness is unmerited. It is not God's response to our seeking him; it is his initiative toward us. Those who will not accept the fact that they are loved and forgiven, consequently, are unable to love. Love cannot be given if it has not been received. Simple as these truths may be, they are the key to the gospel and the life it offers. They are also the deeper locus of most of the problems a pastoral counselor encounters. Unfortunately, simple truths may be the hardest lessons to learn.

The end of vs. 10 links the death of Jesus to the revelation of God's love. It was not just the incarnation which revealed the Father's love; that love was also revealed by Jesus' atoning death. The elder may have needed to drive this point home for the community because they may have emphasized the coming of Jesus (Christmas), neglecting the importance of his death (Easter). The prologue to John, after all, extols the significance of the incarnation but says nothing about the atonement. The elder will not allow emphasis on one without the other; the Father sent his Son as, or to be, an *expiation* for our sins (see the discussion of this term above, 2:2). By his life and death Jesus fulfilled the works of God and revealed his love for us. For that reason the church can never be allowed to forget the Gospel accounts of Jesus' earthly ministry. They tell the story that has the power to give life. They also point us to the source of perfect love.

The Experience of Perfect Love (4:11–16a)

This unit may be divided into two subsections: vss. 11–12 and 13–16a. The first resumes the emphasis of 4:7. Because God has loved us, we ought to love one another. The second subsection turns to the role of faith in the experience of God's love. The sequence of thought, therefore, is not from the reception of God's love to expression of it in love for one another, as in 4:11. Instead, the elder's thought moves from the command to love to that which enables us to do so. Having dealt with the second part of the double command stated in 3:23, he returns in verses 13–16a to the first part, i.e., "believe in his name." Belief is that response to God's love which enables the community to exercise love for one another.

The language of vs. 11 is thoroughly Johannine. *Beloved* occurs here for the last time. "God so loved us" is an echo of John 3:16, already evoked by 4:9. In fact, this section may be a commentary on John 3:16; the outline of the verse can be seen in the emphasis on "God so loved" in 4:11, "gave" and "sent" in 4:13–14, "his Son" in 4:15, and "believing" in 4:16a. The "ought" in 4:11 is similar to that in 2:6 and 3:16. As in these previous references, the "ought," the mandate for Christian life, arises from the revelation of the character of God in the life of Jesus. The word *so* or *thus* refers to the main emphases of the previous verses: God loved us, sent his only Son that we might have life, and sent his Son as an expiation for our sin. God's love was revealed in both the sending of Jesus and in his death. It follows then that we are to love one another, and by this the elder means maintaining the unity and fellowship of the community (unlike the defectors), laying down our lives for one another if necessary (perhaps in the context of persecution; 3:16, John 16:2), and sharing life's goods with those in need (3:17).

In the Gospel of John (1:18; 5:37; 6:46) the assertion that no one had seen God serves to establish Jesus' superiority over Moses or Elijah. The elder repeats that assertion here because he is going on to make the point that God is revealed as he abides in us and as his love is perfected in us. God cannot be seen, but his love is visible in the lives of those in whom he abides. The condition for the indwelling presence of God is that we love one another. From the way vs. 12 is stated one might infer that God cannot dwell in a person who is unwilling or unable to love his or her brothers and sisters in Christ; he does not abide in those who left the community (2:19). Moreover, if we love one another, God's love is perfected in us. Its redemptive task is completed. Originating from the very character of God himself, revealed in the incarnation and atonement, God's love only finds fulfillment as it is demonstrated in the lives of those who respond in faith (see 2:5; 4:17–18).

Verse 13 appeals to the giving of the Spirit as confirmation that we abide in God and he abides in us. This promise of mutual indwelling picks up another emphasis from 3:24, the transitional verse which introduced this part of the epistle. Just as God sent his Son, he has given believers "from his spirit." The same phrase occurs in 3:24, and in both it is a reference to the sending of the Paraclete, the Holy Spirit. The tests of the Spirit were stated in 4:1–6. The emphasis of the phrase is now that the Spirit given to believers is from God's own Spirit, from God himself. Through the Spirit, therefore, God dwells within us.

No one has *seen* God (4:12), but we have seen that the Father sent the Son (4:14). The same verb is used in both verses, and it is the same verb which appears in the epistle's prologue (1:1). The community is the heir of the eyewitness testimony of the Beloved Disciple, who saw and bore witness

(John 19:35; 21:24; see 3:11). Jesus had said that he would reveal himself to his own but the world would not see him (John 14:22), and he had said that the Paraclete would bear witness concerning him (John 15:26). The community, therefore, was authorized by eyewitness testimony (see also John 1:14; 2:11). By bearing witness to the truth that the Father sent Jesus to be "the Savior of the world" (John 4:42; see 1 John 2:2) they carried forward the work of the Paraclete. Bearing witness means above all publicly declaring one's faith in Jesus. The Gospel of John does not accept the faith of those who refuse to declare it openly (John 1:20; 12:42; 19:38). Believing that Jesus is the Son of God (John 20:31) requires public confession. Confession exposed one to the threat of persecution and meant exclusion from the Jewish community (John 9:22; 16:2), but whoever confesses Jesus has fellowship with God (2:23; 4:2–3). Two criteria have been laid down for the indwelling presence of God, the same two as expressed in the double command of 3:23–24: God dwells in those who believe in Jesus as his Son (4:15), and God dwells in those believers who love one another (4:12, 16b). By tying the promise of God's abiding presence to confession of Jesus, the elder has continued the polemical requirement of 4:2—confess Jesus Christ come in flesh.

Verse 16 returns to the primary theme of this paragraph: our experience of God's love. One can know the depth of God's love only by seeing it revealed in the incarnation and death of Jesus. Apart from the confession of Jesus as the Christ, the Son of God, therefore, one cannot know or believe in the fullness of God's love. Such an assertion would be further confirmed for the elder in that the indwelling presence of God, which is essential for his love to be fulfilled *in us*, is possible only through faith in Jesus (4:15; see John 17:26). The experience of God's love, perfected in us, therefore, is what it means to have eternal life. And that is the real meaning of John 3:16.

The Confidence of Perfect Love (4:16b–21)

The third unit of this section picks up the themes of the first two and winds them into a pointed conclusion. Although this meditation on love has defied attempts to divide it into neat units, these last verses in chapter 4 seem to make three points. First, the mutual indwelling of the Christian in God and God in the Christian brings his love to completion (4:16b). Second, the experience of his perfect love produces a fearless confidence in the day of judgment (4:17–18). Third, anyone who claims to love God and yet does not love his or her fellow Christians is a liar (4:19–21). These verses repeat earlier emphases, but they also advance the argument. They enrich the traditional Johannine axioms and draw out the implications of words and phrases which may have been emptied of meaning by overuse.

Verse 16 is the culmination of the theme of abiding. The verb *to abide* does not occur again in 1 John after this verse. Like a masterful symphony, 1 John develops many variations on this theme. Whoever claims to abide in Christ should live as he lived (2:6). One who loves his brother abides in the light (2:10). God's word abides in us (2:14), and whoever does God's will abides forever (2:17). We have an anointing which teaches us all things, therefore abide in what you heard from the beginning (2:24–27). Everyone who abides in Christ does not sin (3:6, 9). On the other hand, one who does not love abides in death (3:14–15). The important verse at the end of the previous section (3:24) capped off the previous development of the theme: if one keeps God's commandments, one experiences the abiding presence of God; and we know that he abides in us because he has given us the Spirit. Repeatedly the elder makes the point that the evidence of God's abiding in the life of a believer is the Christian's love for others (e.g., 3:17). Because of the character of God as one who loves (4:8, 16), he abides in the lives of those for whom Christian love is a way of life. Verse 8 states the negative conclusion, vs. 16 the positive. *Love* in vs. 16 is not indiscriminate or undefined, however. All the rest of 1 John demands that here too the elder has in mind love for fellow believers.

The "in this" in vs. 17 may refer to the preceding statement or to one of the next two clauses. How is God's love perfected with us? By our abiding in him and he in us (vs. 16b), by our being confident in the day of judgment (vs. 17b), or by our being just as he is (vs. 17c)? While each of these alternatives may be argued, the logic is clearest if one takes "in this" as a reference to what precedes and translates the second part of vs. 17 as a result clause. God's love is completed or perfected only when we abide in him and he abides in us. Although the question probably did not trouble the elder, later theologians would want to say that the quality or character of God's love was never imperfect, but its expression, its work, is not perfected until it abides in the lives of his people (see 2:5; 4:12). The result is that we can be confident in the day of judgment. The judge will be the one whose love we have already experienced. Our confidence in God's love allows us to pray to him now (3:21–22; 5:14) and to face the future without fear of judgment (2:28; 4:17). *Judgment* is a familiar Johannine theme, but "the day of judgment" does not occur elsewhere in the Johannine writings. Even the Gospel of John, which emphasizes that judgment occurred in the world's response to Jesus (John 3:19; 5:24; 12:31; 16:11), still recognizes that there is an unfulfilled future dimension of judgment as well (John 5:28–29; 6:39–40). The distinctive Johannine emphasis is that the traditional expectation of judgment on the last day has been realized in the incarnation of Jesus with its sifting of people on the basis of their response to him. The elder's opponents, therefore, had good reason to think that the judgment was already past and that they would face no future judgment. Nevertheless, the elder viewed their eschatology as mistaken and dangerous because it led to neglect of the command to love. The defectors from the Johannine community probably charged that the elder's group had no confidence in God because they still lived in fear of a future judgment. With either surgical precision or baffling paradox, the elder affirms both that we have already been born of God and have crossed over from death into life (3:14) and that there will still be a day of judgment (2:28; 4:17). We must keep God's commands in order to abide in him, but we do have confidence (2:28; 4:17). The elder and his opponents share the same Johannine presuppositions, therefore, but do not draw the same conclusions from them.

The last clause of the sentence (vs. 17) is causal. It explains why we can have confidence in the day of judgment: we have become just as he is. The placement of the phrase "in this world" obscures its sense. Earlier the elder said that we ought to walk *just as that one* (Christ) walked, purify ourselves, and be righteous just as he was (2:6; 3:3, 7). Now he explains the basis for our confidence by saying that just as Christ manifested God's love in the world, so now as children of God in the world we are manifesting his love. We can have confidence because we stand in the same relationship to the Father as Christ did, and we do so by virtue of abiding in him. The Lord's prayer in John 17 has been fulfilled; he keeps his own, protects us from the evil one, and makes us one with him (John 17:11, 15, 21). Our becoming like him, therefore, is not deferred until we see him (3:2). We are already like him, even in this world, because we are his children and his love has been perfected in us.

There are differences among the various Greek texts and commentaries over where to begin vs. 18. These differences go back to the marking of the verse divisions in the sixteenth century. Most translations begin vs. 18 with "there is no fear in love" (RSV). The love in question must be that perfect love whose source is God himself. It is experienced by those who confess Christ, and leads to confidence in the day of judgment. Verse 18, therefore, is not a general observation about the experience of fear in any relationship of love. It is a specific assertion that the present experience of God's love in our lives casts out fear of condemnation at the final judgment. The experience of God's perfect love—his abiding presence in us and the continuing expression of that love in our relationship to fellow Christians—is such that the believer can scarcely fear that he will condemn us for our sins. He is the God we have come to know through the life and death of Christ. We may be confident, therefore, that he has forgiven, does forgive us when we confess our sins (1:9), and will not condemn us on that day.

On the other hand, "fear has to do with punishment" (RSV, NIV, TEV), or "fear involves punishment" (NASB; see KJV, ASV). Those who live in dread and fear of God are those who walk in darkness. They have not come to know God and are already experiencing an estrangement from God which is a foretaste of their eternal punishment. Other passages of Scripture speak of a fear of God which is appropriate for his people, but not 1 John. Those who fear God, i.e., fear his rejection and judgment, have not experienced his love. They have not been perfected by God's love and are therefore still in danger of his judgment. It is precisely the origin and experience of perfect love (God's love) which allows us to be confident of deliverance from judgment. The experience of God's love frees us from fear. Death no longer needs to be seen as entrance into the unknown. By our knowledge of God, who stands also on the other side of death, we have already crossed from death into life. We are free to live in his fellowship now, free from anxiety over both guilt and death. This meditation on love may have been meant to reassure the Johannine Christians troubled by the charges of their opponents, but it is also a profound statement of the meaning of salvation.

The last three verses (19–21) return to the command to love one another, the command with which this section began (4:7). Following the exploration of perfect love's origin, experience, and confidence, therefore, the elder comes once again to the imperative of love.

The opening words of vs. 19 may be translated either as "let us love" or as "we love." The latter is preferable both from the tone of the context and from the emphatic position of the pronoun *we*. The verse repeats in briefer fashion what was stated earlier in 4:10. We are capable of *agape* because we have experienced it in the sending and sacrifice of God's Son. That love, as the next verse will show, can be expressed both in our relationship to God and in our relationship to one another. But we need not be anxious over whether we have been good enough to earn God's love; he loved us first, even before we responded to him (see John 3:16 again).

Verse 20 returns to a formula similar to those used earlier in the letter for quoting the opponents: "If anyone says ..." (1:6, 8, 10; 2:4, 6, 9). The elder is probably thinking of the opponents again. It is not the claim to love God that is objectionable; it is their lack of love for their fellow Christians. There is no middle ground in Johannine dualism, as we have seen. Lack of love can only be construed as hate, and one who hates his brother is in darkness (2:9, 11) and is a murderer (3:15). These last references are tantamount to saying that one who hates his brother does not know God and is in fact of the devil (see John 8:44). It is axiomatic, therefore, that one who does not love his or her fellow Christians cannot claim to love God. That person is a liar, like those who claim to know God but do not keep his commandments (2:4), or those who deny that Jesus is the Christ (2:22). Lack of love exposes not just a moral flaw; it shows that one has not experienced God's love.

A person who cannot love a brother, whose need he has seen (see 3:17), certainly cannot love God, whom he has not seen (see 4:12). The elder's point is that his opponents, who do not love the Johannine Christians, have shown thereby that they do not love God either. This statement reasons from the lesser to the greater, from the easier to the more difficult. It may also arise from a more profound understanding of the nature of love. If God is love and has revealed his nature through his love for us, then if we do not love one another we reveal that we have never received his love. We cannot claim a personal individualistic faith that involves only our relationship to God. His love will not tolerate such limits. Only those who give of themselves for the well-being of others can claim to love God. The elder thought only of the imperative to love one's fellow Christians, but ultimately God's love will not tolerate that limitation either, as other NT witnesses verify.

The second element of the double command in 3:23 is repeated at the end of this chapter in a slightly different form: "he who loves God should love his brother also" (4:21, RSV). The elder will return to the command to believe in the next chapter. This concluding verse is milder than the previous one, but it is the only conclusion to which a discussion of perfect love can come. God's love is completed and perfected in our love for one another. The greatest gift we can give in return for the love he has shown us in his Son Jesus Christ is to love one another in his name. His command is itself an extension of his love, for in fulfilling it we show his love to others, and in the process come to know him more perfectly. That is both the nature of perfect love and its imperative. That love originates from God, from his very being, and builds community between us and others and us and him, drawing us together and revealing in the process the nature of that life to which he has called us.

"Perfect Love" is a natural theme for a variety of sermons which can explore the relationship of God's love to Christian love for others. Attractive sermon topics come easily—"First Love, Finest Love," "Love's Counterfeits," "Casting Out Fear"—but successful sermon preparation will depend on avoiding sentimental piety and keeping the subject related to the difficult task of integrating our relationship to God with our relationships to others.

The Essentials of Faith
(1 John 5:1–12)

This section gathers up the main themes of the epistle and relates them to the nature of faith. It is the last section of the body of the epistle, followed only by the conclusion (5:13–21). There is considerable debate over where to begin and end this section, but I have chosen these limits because of the internal indicators which mark the beginning and ending of three distinct units within the section.

  I. Faith, Love Leading to Victory (5:1–4)
     5:1 Everyone who believes that Jesus is the Christ
     5:4 This is the victory
 II. Faith, The Testimony of Three Witnesses (5:5–9)
     5:5 ...the one who believes that Jesus is the Son of God
     5:9 This is the testimony
III. Faith, God's Testimony Expressed in Life (5:10–12)
     5:10 One who believes in the Son of God
     5:11 This is the life

Verse 1 reintroduces the theme of faith (or believing), which serves as a unifying theme for this section. Of the nine occurrences of the verb "to believe" in 1 John, five are in this section, one in the next verse (5:13), and the others in 3:23, 4:1, and 4:16. Each of the units in this section features the phrase "one who believes" in the opening verse (5:1, 5, 10). The end of each unit is marked by the statement "this is. . . ." The significance of this pattern is diminished by the repetition of this formula elsewhere in these verses (vss. 3, 6, 11a) and by the fact that in the third unit the formula is clarified by a further statement in vs. 12. Structural patterns are seldom entirely regular in 1 John, as we have seen, but these two clauses do appear to mark the beginnings and endings of the three units in this section.

The first unit relates believing to the imperative of love, which was the theme of the preceding section of 1 John (4:7–21). Because 5:1b–3 continue and in some respects conclude the earlier emphasis, many commentators interpret 5:1–4 as the conclusion of 4:7–21. It is characteristic of 1

John to use transitional verses to move from one theme to another, however, and the following factors all favor treating 5:1–4 as the introduction to this section: (1) the pattern of introductions and conclusions in the three units (5:1–4, 5–9, and 10–12), (2) the reappearance of the first part of the double command, "believe in his name" (3:23) in 5:1, and (3) the fact that 4:7–21 is already longer than any other section of the epistle. The end of the section is indicated both by the pattern sketched above and by the first-person reference to the act of writing in 5:13, which introduces the conclusion of the letter. Alternatively, vs. 13 could be viewed as the concluding verse of this section with no great change of meaning.

The first unit within this section promises that everyone who believes has been born of God. Therefore loving one's brothers and sisters is integral to the life of faith, through which believers share in Christ's victory. The second unit is concerned with the content of faith, which is defined by the testimony of the three witnesses—the Spirit, the water, and the blood. The third unit affirms that the believer has God's testimony; and that testimony, ultimately, is the life he has given us. By this progression, the elder ties together most of the central concerns of the letter: the essentials of faith, the Christology required by faith, the brotherhood of believers as the children of God, the new commandment, and the nature of the life the believers already enjoy.

Faith, Love Leading to Victory (5:1–4)

The first part of vs. 1 repeats an axiom of the Johannine Christians' self-understanding: "Everyone who believes that Jesus is the Christ has been born of God." Here, as elsewhere in 1 John, *believe* is used in relation to statements about Jesus (4:1 is followed by 4:2, and 4:16 is derived from 4:9–10). The basis for this axiom lies at the center of the prologue to the Gospel of John: "But to all who received him, who believed in his name, he gave authority to become the children of God" (1:12). Through the response of faith, believers are born from above (John 3:3); they participate in the life which Jesus promised to his own. This faith is now qualified by the elder's requirement that they confess "Jesus Christ come in flesh" (4:2).

All of the previous uses of the verb *to beget* or *to be born* (passive) have also described believers (2:29; 3:9; 4:7; see 5:4, 18), which is important for the interpretation of the second half of vs. 1. "Everyone who loves the parent loves the child" is probably a traditional aphorism. In this context it is used to make a point, but is it related to the first part of the verse or to the next verse (vs. 2)? Is the child here Christ or the Christian? Probably the latter. The elder is building toward the same conclusion he has drawn before: the faithful can tell who has been born of God by seeing who shows love for their fellow Christians. One who lives in fellowship with God will inevitably love others who share in this fellowship. The implication, therefore, is that the opponents have not been born of God.

The aphorism in vs. 1 raises a problem. How does one know when he or she is loving the children of God? No doubt those who left the community loved one another and claimed that they were fulfilling the new commandment. The elder responds with another Johannine principle: "In this. . . ." The rest of the verse comes close to summing up the elder's understanding of the imperative of the gospel: love God and do his commandments. Verse 2 is therefore the Johannine equivalent of the Jewish *Shema* (Deut 6:4–9) and the command to love one's neighbor (Lev 19:18). *Agape* comes from God, so we can love his children only when we love him— and only a hypocrite or liar would claim to love him and not do as he commanded. Typical of the narrow circle within which the elder's logic moves, God's commands are above all to believe in Jesus (John 14:1; 1 John 5:1) and to love one another (John 13:34; 1 John 4:7–21), both of which were repeated in 3:23.

Verse 3 demands that professions of love for God be accompanied by obedience to his commands. The opponents no doubt claimed to love God, but at least in the eyes of the elder they did not take seriously the need for obedience to his commands. The elder allows no room for private mystical experiences of love for God that do not affect the way in which the Christian lives and relates to others. Both God's love for us and our love for God are perfected by obedience to his commands (see 2:5; John 14:15; 15:10). The statement that God's commands are not "heavy," burdensome or difficult, runs deep in the biblical tradition (Deut 30:11; Matt 11:30). In this context, the point is no doubt connected with the earlier statements that the one who gave the commands also gave of his Spirit (3:23–24) and we are able to love— which is the essence of his commands—because he first loved us (4:19). The simple truth is, it is easy to love when we are loved. More profoundly, *agape* is impossible for those who do not know God, but comes naturally for those who have been transformed by his love.

The unit ends with the assurance of victory, which makes it attractive for sermonic use. In Johannine dualism there is only that which belongs to God and that which belongs to the world. Here the elder chooses a neuter rather than a masculine pronoun to emphasize that all who belong to God will share in his victory over the world. The elder has already said that the young men have conquered the evil one (2:13, 14), and the community has overcome the false prophets (4:4). Through faith in Jesus as the Christ, public profession of the faith, exclusion of the false prophets, and love for one another, they were participating in Jesus' victory over the world (John 16:33). "Our faith" is therefore victory in itself, and all who love God may be assured that by exercising his love in the world, Christ's victory is being achieved. Love is vanquishing hate; darkness is giving way to light, falsehood to truth, and iniquity to righteousness. But it takes faith to see the victory assured.

Faith leads to love, and love is the "Path to Victory." Alternatively, "When Faith Is a Victory" might serve as a sermon title, but care should be taken to define the context of the struggle and the meaning of *victory* so that the preacher does not simply feed the church's natural inclination toward triumphalism.

Faith, the Testimony of Three Witnesses (5:5–9)

For the elder not all faith is victorious. The defectors from the Johannine community believed, but their faith was defective and inauthentic. Consequently, the content of victorious faith must be defined. Earlier the elder had asked, "Who is the liar if not the one who denies that Jesus is the Christ?" (2:22). Now he reverses the question: "who is the one who conquers the world if not the one who believes that Jesus is

the Son of God?" They are conquering the world because the
one in them (Christ) is greater than the power in the world
(the devil). *Conquering* is a recurrent theme in the seven letters in Revelation; all who hold to the faith will receive eternal life. There are eight references to Jesus as the Son in
5:5–13, more than in any other section of the epistle. The title
was introduced in the prologue (1:3), however, and recurs in
other sections (1:7; 2:22–24; 3:8, 23; 4:9, 10, 14, 15; 5:20). The
content of victorious faith is therefore preeminently christological. It affirms that *Jesus* is the Son of God, and emphasis
on his earthly life may be implied.

Verse 6 continues this emphasis, but is notorious for its
ambiguity. The problem is not broken grammar or lack of
clarity but our inability to determine the precise nuances
water and *blood* would have had for the Johannine Christians. Several interpretations have been advanced by commentators: (1) *water* refers to Jesus' birth or his baptism and
blood refers to his death; (2) together they emphasize the incarnation; (3) together they emphasize Jesus' death; (4) *water*
refers to baptism, *blood* refers to the eucharist. As popular as
the sacramental interpretation has been in some circles, the
context dictates that here *water* and *blood* must validate the
manner of Jesus' *coming*, a verb used of Jesus elsewhere in 1
John only in 4:2, "come in flesh." *Blood*, moreover, was
clearly associated with Jesus' death (1:7), and the elder has
been concerned to stress the redemptive significance of the
death (2:2). It is unlikely, therefore, that the emphasis is on
the incarnation exclusively. Ruling out alternatives 2 and 4
leaves one still with the question of whether the elder was
opposing the beliefs that later came to be called Docetism.
Cerinthus, the most famous proponent of Docetism, taught
that Jesus received the divine Spirit at his baptism and gave
it up before he died. Commentators once suggested that Cerinthus was the elder's opponent, but it now appears more
likely that Cerinthus refined and gave classic expression to
the views of the elder's opponents a generation or two after 1
John was written. Alternatively, the elder may have been
striving to correct the view that only the incarnation was
redemptively significant. The death of Jesus, according to
such a view, was simply Jesus' return to the Father, his exaltation, which was the culmination of the incarnation. This

latter view could easily be derived from the Gospel of John, which emphasizes the incarnation in the prologue and then treats the death of Jesus, contrary to the Synoptic Gospels, as Jesus' enthronement and exaltation. Was the issue the reality of the incarnation (Docetism) or the significance of Jesus' death (soteriology)? The assertion "not in the water only but in the water and the blood" lays the emphasis on Jesus' death, but one could hedge his or her bet by pointing out that (1) whether the issue was Docetism or soteriology, this verse points to the importance of Jesus' death, and (2) the reality of the incarnation, which was clearly a Johannine theme (see 1:1; John 1:14), also had soteriological significance for the elder.

If the prologue was a late addition to the Gospel of John, as is often suggested, the Gospel may once have begun with John the Baptist's testimony that the Spirit descended upon Jesus when he was baptized. He was therefore the Son of God, the Lamb of God who takes away the sin of the world (John 1:29–34). Apart from the eucharistic language of John 6:53–56, the Gospel does not mention blood except in the verse where it also appears with water: when one of the soldiers pierced Jesus' side "there came out blood and water" (19:34). 1 John 5:6 reverses the sequence, "water and blood," which may suggest that the sequence of baptism and then death is intended. Water was associated with cleansing, life, and the Spirit, as may be seen from study of the relevant Johannine passages (John 1:26, 31, 33; 2:7–9; 3:5, 8; 4:10–15; 7:38; 13:5). In John's account of Jesus' death, all three of the witnesses cited in 1 John 5:6–8 are mentioned: water, blood, and Spirit. Fulfilling John 7:38–39, water flows from Jesus' side and he hands over the Spirit (John 19:30). The Beloved Disciple saw and bore witness (John 19:35; see 1 John 5:6). The Johannine church had heard the truth from the Beloved Disciple, and the elder no doubt assumed that the Spirit was guiding him. Any faith which diminished the significance of Jesus' death, even if it affirmed the incarnation, was deficient, even deceptive and satanic, because the importance of the death of Jesus was confirmed by the three witnesses, which included the Spirit of Truth.

The three witnesses (vs. 8) fulfill the prescription of Deut 19:15 (see John 8:17), and they continue to bear witness, both through the gospel story and through the believer's experience of baptism, the eucharist, and the anointing of the Spirit (2:27).

A famous insertion, the so-called Johannine Comma, occurs at the end of vs. 7 (or the middle of vs. 8, RSV). In the Latin manuscript tradition the words "in heaven: Father, Word, and Holy Spirit; and these three are one; and there are three who testify on earth" were inserted beginning in the fourth century in manuscripts which come from North Africa and Spain. The Johannine Comma does not appear in any Greek manuscript before A.D. 1400, and is now recognized as a gloss motivated by the trinitarian debates of the fourth and fifth centuries.

Verse 8 continues with the solemn, almost liturgical, assertion that the three witnesses are one. They are all in agreement. If the sacramental associations of *water* and *blood* are now more prominent than they were in vs. 6, where the immediate reference was to the death and possibly the baptism of Jesus, then the elder is affirming that the community's experience of these observances and the continuing presence of the Spirit bear witness to the content of faith. Specifically, the three witnesses confirm the truth of the elder's teachings. On the other hand, if the elder's opponents had once belonged to the Johannine community, what might they have believed about baptism and the Lord's Supper? Following the earlier indications that they thought they were beyond the possibility of sinning, they may have viewed the sacraments as almost magical in their power to protect believers. Paul warned the Corinthians against such a view (1 Cor 10:1–22), and Ignatius of Antioch spoke of the eucharist as "the medicine of immortality" *(Ephesians* 20.2). It is difficult to detect a polemic against a false view of the sacraments in 1 John, however. The continuing witness of Spirit, water, and blood is important because these testify to the importance of Jesus' redemptive death (see 1:7; 2:2).

The structure of vs. 9 is far from clear. It obviously contrasts human testimony with God's testimony, possibly with the implication that the opponents accept the former but not the latter. Beyond this the verse is open to several interpretations. The reference to human testimony probably does not have a specific witness (e.g., John the Baptist) in mind. More

likely, it is a general reference to the practice of accepting the
testimony of two or three witnesses, as specified by law, or to
accepting the testimony of recognized leaders or prophets.
Clearly, God's testimony should be accorded greater value,
but what is God's testimony? Presumably the elder assumed
that the testimony of the Spirit, if not also the water and the
blood, was God's testimony. Hence, vs. 9 follows naturally
from the previous verse. The second part of vs. 9 contains
two clauses which begin with *hoti*, which can be translated
either as a causal conjunction (for, because, since) or as a
substantive (that). Either way, vs. 9 does not explain what
God's testimony is. It merely asserts that God has borne testimony to his Son, as the Gospel of John says (5:32, 37). The
meaning of God's testimony in the experience of believers
will be interpreted further in the next three verses.

Faith, God's Testimony Expressed in Life (5:10–12)

God's testimony to his Son, cited in the previous verses but
not explained, now becomes the theme which unifies vss.
10–12. "The one who believes in the Son of God" has been
born of God (5:1), conquers the world (5:5), and has God's
testimony in himself (5:10). That testimony, therefore, is in-
terior and self-authenticating. The Gospel of John makes
similar affirmations. One who believes has authority to become a child of God (1:12), and does not perish but has eternal life (3:15, 16, 18, 36; 5:24; 6:40, 47; 11:25, 26). The
believer will never thirst (6:35), does not abide in darkness
(12:46), and will also do the works which Jesus did (14:12).
John 3:33 declared that whoever accepts Jesus' testimony
has certified that God is true. The elder now makes the point
negatively: one who does not believe God's testimony has
made him a liar (see 1:10). God's testimony is embodied in
Jesus and conveyed by him. One who rejects Jesus has therefore rejected God's testimony, in effect declaring the testimony false and the witness a liar (see John 3:18).

The body of 1 John began with the words "and this is the
message" (1:5). It ends with the formula "and this is the testimony" (5:11). That testimony, God's testimony, is that he
has given us eternal life. Jesus conveyed the testimony, and it
is self-evident in the experience of the believer. That life,

moreover, is a testimony to the character and ultimate purpose of all God's creative and redemptive works. The ambiguous appeal to God's testimony in vs. 9 is therefore finally
clarified. The final appeal is to the believer's experience of
that life which God gives to those who respond to him in
faith. All Johannine Christians would agree that life can
come only through Jesus (John 1:4; 5:26, 40; 6:35, 48; 10:28;
11:25; 14:6; 17:3). Through believing in Jesus, the believer
"has" Jesus, but 1 John also maintains that the believer has
all of the following: fellowship with other believers (1:7), a
Paraclete before the Father (2:1), the new command (2:7;
4:21), an anointing (2:20), the Father (2:23), confidence
before God (2:28; 3:21; 4:17; 5:14), hope (3:3), God's testimony (5:10), and above all eternal life (5:12–13). One who
does not believe does not have the Son and therefore cannot
have eternal life.

The body of 1 John ends with the promise of life, just as the
Gospel of John does (20:30–31; see 1 John 5:13). This last
section of the body of the letter defines the elder's view of
faith as believing in Jesus. Such faith, genuine faith, produces profound changes, for the believer is "born of God."
Love comes naturally to the children of God. Through their
faith believers also share in Christ's victory and conquer the
world. The christological content required of true faith is
conveyed in the testimony of three witnesses—the Spirit, the
water, and the blood. To these God adds his own testimony,
which is self-authenticating because it is that life which only
God can give, and it is given only through Jesus, his Son.
Genuine faith is therefore validated by love which is ultimately victorious, by testimony to the saving significance of
Jesus' death, and by life lived in fellowship with other believers and with God himself. These three points can serve as the
basic structure for a sermon entitled "When Faith Becomes
Genuine." Eternal life is the fulfillment of God's being, his
love for us, and his redemptive work. Faith, also, is self-authenticating, but only for believers. These are truths the
world cannot grasp.

The Certainties of Faith
(1 John 5:13–21)

The concluding verses call the readers to the certainties of their faith. Attention to the essentials of true faith in the previous section now allows the elder to take stock of those verities assured by faith. In the face of threat the community will do well to remember those things in which it can have confidence.

The theme of certainty is set from the beginning. Verse 13, which resembles closely the conclusion of the Gospel of John (20:30–31), begins, "I have written these things to you in order that you may *know.*" Verse 14 speaks of the confidence we have, and vs. 15 reasons, "If we know, . . . then we know. . . ." The verb *we know* becomes the unifying refrain of vss. 18–20, since it is the first word in each of those verses.

Verses 16–17 and 21 do not fit the theme or tone of confidence. The matter of praying for forgiveness for a brother's sin must be clarified. There are some instances, the elder says, when the faithful are not to pray for forgiveness. These verses must be understood in the context of Johannine thought. The concluding verse also seems out of place: "Little children, guard yourselves from the idols." Since idolatry has not been mentioned as a problem, metaphorical interpretations must be considered.

Verse 13 introduces the conclusion with its shift to the first person, its reference to the writing of the epistle, and its emphasis on knowing. References to Jesus as the Son of God in vss. 13 and 20 form a frame for the conclusion. Within these concluding verses two units can be identified: vss. 13–17 and vss. 18–21, although vs. 21 could be treated in isolation. The verbs for knowing and having cement vss. 13–15 together. Verses 16–17 are treated as a caveat or clarification rather than as a separate unit. The conclusion, then, reminds readers of both the confidence they have in prayer and the confidence they have in God's protection.

Confidence in Prayer (5:13–17)

The elder has often said "I am writing" (2:1, 7, 8, 12, 13; see 1:4) or "I have written these things" (2:13, 14, 21, 26). Here his reference to what he has written probably embraces not just the preceding verses but the entire epistle. Just as John 20:31 states the purpose for the writing of the Gospel, so 5:13 states the purpose of the epistle. Verse 13 also forms a frame with the conclusion of the epistle's prologue:

> 1 John 5:13 I write this to you who believe in the name of the Son of God, that you may know that you have eternal life.
>
> John 20:31 But these are written that you may believe that Jesus is the Christ, the Son of God, and that believing you may have life in his name.
>
> 1 John 1:4 And we are writing this that our joy may be complete. (RSV)

The similarities, especially with the Gospel's purpose statement, are obvious. The elder may have patterned vs. 13 after that statement simply out of familiarity with it or deliberately to evoke the authority of the Gospel. Both the Gospel and the epistle were probably written to explain the nature of faith. The epistle was clearly written to those who were already Christians, and written to warn them against those who would corrupt their faith. The readers should know, therefore, that they already have life. Such certainty would be their best defense against the false teachings of those who left the community.

The syntax of vs. 13 is fractured; the phrase "to those who believe" comes at the end, as it does in John 1:12 (see 1 John 5:16). As the elder emphasized in the preceding verses, eternal life comes through believing in God's Son. This conclusion repeats the epistle's call for faith, a call which is stated only in the second half of the epistle (3:23; 5:1, 5, 10, 13). Believing *in the name* of the Son of God distinguishes the Johannine Christians (John 1:12), and for the elder it must mean believing in the Christ who has come *in flesh* (4:2). To believe in the name of Jesus means therefore to stake one's life on his ministry and death and to live under the ethic of righteousness and love, as he commanded. Such faith makes fellowship complete (1:4). Through the name of Jesus forgive-

ness for sin is also available (2:12), so the elder turns to the
confidence in prayer which is part of authentic faith.

Where the elder speaks of confidence it is always confidence before God: confidence in the day of judgment (2:28;
4:17) and confidence in the hour of prayer (3:21–22; 5:14).
Confident prayer can only come from those who know God as
their Father and know themselves as his children. Their confidence is that God will hear them whenever they ask according to his will. The emphasis on confidence in prayer is not
new, but comes from the Gospel. Jesus was confident that the
Father always heard him (John 11:42), and even the Jews in
the Gospel affirm that God hears those who do his will (John
9:31). Moreover, Jesus told his disciples that whatever they
asked in his name they would receive (John 14:13–14; 15:7,
16; 16:23–24, 26–27). Jesus would be the advocate for the
faithful (2:1); but if God has already given us life (5:13), then
it is a far lesser thing that he should also answer when we
call upon him with particular needs. The stated assumption
is that God's children will ask according to his will. The only
other reference to doing God's will in 1 John is in 2:17, where
the assurance is given that those who do his will abide forever. Jesus repeatedly said that his mission was only to do
the will of the one who sent him (John 4:34; 5:30), specifically, giving eternal life to those who believe (John 6:38–40).
Doing God's will therefore means continuing and extending
Jesus' redemptive work, and that through being righteous
and loving others with the kind of love we have experienced
from him (see 2:29; 4:7–12).

Hearing in the Johannine writings often means privileged
communication. The Son hears the Father (John 5:30; 8:26,
40; 15:15). The sheep hear the shepherd's voice (John10:3,
16), and those who believe hear Jesus' words (John 12:47;
14:28; 18:37). Others cannot hear (John 5:37; 8:43, 47; 9:27).
The elder refers often to what his readers had heard from the
beginning (1:1, 3, 5, etc.), the word of life, the tradition of the
Johannine school, the new command, the gospel. He also
says that the world hears those who have gone out from the
community (4:5). Those who know God hear "us" (4:6). Now
he adds the ultimate privilege, which is also the ultimate assurance that one has fellowship with God: God hears us. That
certainty is a shield against false teaching and a bulwark

against despair. Hope and confidence can always thrive when one knows that God listens to his children.

The confidence which Martha expressed to Jesus, "whatever you ask from God, God will give you" (John 11:22), the elder expressed to the community. The children of God all share the intimacy of communication which Jesus had with the Father. Verse 15 repeats this assurance in redundant fashion, adding answered prayer to the inventory of things the faithful have (see the discussion of 5:12). Confidence that we are heard means that we can be confident that we have that for which we have prayed. Again the assumption must be "according to his will," but the logic of vs. 15 is based on the premise that God is faithful (1:9). Apart from God's faithfulness there could be no certainty at all.

Having introduced the topic of prayer in vss. 14 and 15 and stressed the assurance of answered prayer, the elder turns to the specific and delicate matter of prayer for the forgiveness of sins. For the Johannine Christians this may have been a difficult subject because of their insistence on the ideal of perfection (3:6, 9). The elder has maintained, however, that if they would confess their sin, God, who is faithful and just, would forgive them (1:9); and if any of them should sin, Jesus was their expiation (2:1–2). Therefore, if any Christian should see a brother or sister committing a sin "not unto death," he or she should ask forgiveness for that person. Both the cast and the plot are obscure in vs. 16. What is the sin "not unto death"? Clearly such sin may be committed by the faithful; but if one prays, who gives life, and to whom is it given? Does the one who prays thereby give life, or does God give life? Is life given to the one who prays for a brother or sister or to the one who has sinned? In spite of these ambiguities the apparent meaning is fairly clear. Ultimately only God can give life (see John 5:26), but through intercessory prayer the Christian can have a role in restoring an erring brother or sister.

The more difficult issue is the distinction between sin "unto death" and sin "not unto death." The believer can commit a sin not unto death. Could a believer also commit a sin unto death? Even though the lesser sin can be forgiven, the statement "and he will give him life" suggests that life is at least threatened by all sin. The elder has written that the believers have "crossed from death into life" (3:14). Nowhere does he say that those who have left the community have returned from life into death, though he says they are children of the devil (3:10). Instead, the answer is that they never really belonged to the community (2:19); they had never crossed from death into life. The elder is concerned that other members of the community not be lost to the defectors, but it is not clear whether in Johannine theology a believer could commit the sin unto death. If one were to do so, the response would probably be that he or she was never really a believer.

Distinctions among sins were already common in the first century. The OT deals more harshly with deliberate sin, committed "with a high hand," than with inadvertent sin (Lev. 4:1–3; Num 15:22–31; Deut 17:12). The Pharisees distinguished between "light" and "heavy" matters, and the Essenes at Qumran imposed penalties varying with the seriousness of the sin. Some Qumran members could even be cut off from the community permanently (*Community Rule* 7:18–25). The early church similarly distinguished among sins (Matt 18:15–17; Luke 12:47–48; 1 Cor 5:1–5). Some sins, like that of Ananias and Sapphira (Acts 5:1–11) or those referred to by Paul in 1 Cor 11:30, could result in physical death. Blaspheming against the Holy Spirit was also regarded as unforgivable (Mark 3:28–29; Luke 12:10). Hebrews warns against an apostasy for which there could be no restoration (6:4–6; 10:26–27). The distinction in 1 John 5:16 is probably drawn within the context of the Johannine setting. The language is characteristically Johannine. *Death* therefore refers to a spiritual rather than a physical condition; i.e., separation from the life which is only available in Christ. Sin is refusal to believe in Jesus (John 16:8–9). Those who refuse to believe are without excuse (John 15:22) and will die in their sin (John 8:21, 24). The sin "unto death" is therefore refusal to believe in Jesus as the Christ come in flesh (1 John 4:2). Because the elder's opponents would not offer an acceptable confession of faith in Jesus as the Christ and did not love the community, they were cut off from Christ, the giver of life. Their sin had brought them to death, so the elder admonishes the faithful not to pray for such persons. In imposing this restriction, which many find objectionable, the elder was being consistent with the tradition of the Gospel of John. Jesus would not pray for the world (John 17:9), so the elder advises the faithful that they are not to pray for those who belong to the world (1 John 4:5).

Verse 17 treads between two unacceptable attitudes toward sin: one which holds that minor sins are of no consequence, and one which holds that there can be no forgiveness for sin. Although sin can be forgiven, the elder is concerned that it never be taken lightly. All sin, regardless of how minor, is unrighteousness and therefore intolerable for a righteous God or any of his people (see 2:29; 3:4). On the other hand, not all sins place one beyond the possibility of forgiveness, contrary to what some of the Johannine Christians may have thought. The Christian cannot accept any sin, but should pray for forgiveness for oneself and for others.

The primary distinction in vss. 16 and 17 is therefore not between types of sin but between persons for whom one should pray. Pray for fellow Christians who have fallen into sin. Do not pray for those who have refused to believe in Christ. The elder's reasons for imposing such a restriction are understandable: the defectors did not acknowledge their sin; there could be no forgiveness outside of Christ; and some of the faithful might be drawn into sympathy with the defectors by praying for them. Nevertheless, his dualism has led to a restriction which most interpreters have felt must be qualified by more moderate, compassionate, and optimistic pronouncements elsewhere in the NT. C. H. Dodd, for example, wrote, "Upon the ground of the general teaching of the Gospels, and of the New Testament as a whole, and in agreement with the general sense of the Church, we may take leave to accept the affirmation [about prayer] and to ignore the qualification. We cannot think that it can ever be contrary to the will of Him who came to call sinners to repentance that we should pray for even the worst of sinners (who may after all be—ourselves)" (*The Johannine Epistles*, p. 137). The point to be seized upon is surely the admonition that we pray for other Christians who are struggling with sin and may want— desperately—to find forgiveness. For such persons intercessory prayer, and the assurance that they are being prayed for, may be the very sign of acceptance which will prove liberating. If prayer is commanded (by the future tense "he will pray"), can the Christian do less?

Confidence in God's Protection (5:18–21)

The closing verses of the epistle offer three assurances, continuing the theme announced in 5:13—"I have written these things to you so that you may know that you have eternal life." The structure of the conclusion is marked by the repetition of *we know* at the beginning of vss. 18, 19, and 20. The claims to knowing form a familiar refrain. Verbs meaning "to know" occur forty times in 1 John: *ginosko* twenty-five times, and *oida* fifteen times. Here, at the end, they confirm the believer's guarantees, faith's security.

First, the faithful are assured that the children of God do not sin, because the Son of God protects them. Second, the community is assured that it belongs to God, in contrast to the world which lies in the power of the evil one. Third, they are assured that they have the discernment of truth, which has been given to them by the Son of God. Assurance, protection, and the confession that Jesus is the Son of God are the vital themes of these verses. Finally, because they know the only true God through Jesus Christ, the community is warned to guard itself from "the idols."

The first part of vs. 18 repeats the assurance of sinlessness which was first stated in 3:6, 9. Just as those verses are preceded in 1 John by the exhortation to the faithful to confess their sin (in 1:6—2:2), so here the assurance in 5:18 follows the exhortation in 5:16 to pray for fellow believers who have sinned. The elder lives between the reality of sin in the lives of believers and the certainty that sin is alien to the life of God's children. Those who have been born of God practice righteousness (2:29) and love (4:7). They believe that Jesus is the Christ (5:1) and thereby overcome the world (5:4). They cannot sin because God's "seed" abides in them (see the discussion of 3:9).

"The one who was born of God" also keeps them. Numerous interpretations of this phrase have been proposed. Most translations and commentators conclude that it is a reference to Jesus. Raymond Brown and others have contended that neither the Gospel of John nor the Epistles ever speak of Jesus as the one born of God. The verb is used only of believers with the exception of a reference to Jesus' human birth in John 18:37. The meaning, they contend, is that the believer either protects himself or is protected by other believers, perhaps through intercessory prayer (5:16). Interpreting this phrase as an assurance that the children of God are protected by Jesus is still preferable, however, for the following reasons: (1) in the Gospel of John, Jesus never speaks of the disciples' "keeping" one another; he has kept them and prays that the Father may also keep them (John 17:11, 12, 15). (2) The change of tenses in which we encounter the verb *to be born*, from the perfect to the aorist, may signal a change in meaning. This is the only place in 1 John where the verb occurs in the aorist tense (except 5:1, where it may also refer to Jesus) and the only place where it seems to refer to Jesus. (3) The title "Son of God" is emphasized in vs. 20. (4) Jesus is more nearly the counterpart of the evil one (mentioned in 5:18, 19) in Johannine theology. The promise that Jesus protects us is also a much stronger assurance than the promise that we protect ourselves or that we are protected by other believers. Because of this protection, the evil one cannot touch, or hold, the Christian. As the elder has already said, "he who is in you is greater than he who is in the world" (4:4).

The first assurance leads to the second (vs. 19). The elder has assured his readers repeatedly that they belong to God (3:19, 24; 4:4, 6, 13). This assurance may have been necessary because of the doubts created by those who had left the community. They may even have used the elder's insistence on the need to confess sin as an opportunity to say that those who did so showed that they did not really belong to God yet. "The world," on the other hand, meaning all unbelievers and all that pertains to unbelief, lies under the power of the evil one. The faithful, therefore, should not love the world (2:15–17). The world does not understand them (3:1, 13). Cain is an example of one who belonged to the evil one (see 3:10, 12). The world knows neither righteousness nor love, but the children of God have the confidence of having overcome the world (5:4).

The third assurance, vs. 20, is the longest and most involved. First, it affirms that the Son of God has come. That is the basic Christian confession, and echoes John 20:31 and many verses earlier in 1 John (e.g., 4:15). Attention is again focused on the fact of his coming and his revelation of God rather than on his death and resurrection. This emphasis is also characteristic of the prologues to John and 1 John. The statement "he has given us understanding in order that we might know the true one (i.e., God)" is little more than a restatement of John 1:18—Jesus was the revealer of God. It also echoes John 17:3, "And this is eternal life, that they know thee the only true God, and Jesus Christ whom thou hast sent" (RSV). It is not surprising, then, that the elder proceeds to link knowledge of God through Jesus with eternal life in the rest of vs. 20. The essential quality of such life is fellowship with God. As was noted earlier (see the discussion of 2:3–11), 1 John maintains that the new covenant of Jer 31:33–34 has been fulfilled through the revelation and forgiveness of sins mediated by Jesus Christ. More than just knowing God, we are in him as we are in his Son Jesus (see 2:5, 24). The unity for which Jesus prayed (John 17:21) has been realized. He is the way to the Father, to truth and life (John 14:6, 9); apart from the Son one cannot have the Father (2:23).

The final affirmation, while clearly climactic, is nevertheless ambiguous: "This is the only true God and eternal life!" C. H. Dodd contended that the writer is now gathering together "all that he has been saying about God" (Dodd, p. 140). Others (Brown, Marshall) maintain that following the rules of grammar, it refers to the last named person: Jesus. If so, the epistle ends with a high confession of Jesus' deity, just as does the Gospel of John (20:28). At least it is clear that in the writer's thinking, Jesus is the revelation of the only true God, and he is the one in whom we have eternal life (again, see John 17:3). In that sense Jesus is eternal life, much as the epistle's prologue said (1:2). In Jesus that life was made manifest, and he was himself the giver of eternal life.

The last verse is totally unexpected. The author has not used the address "little children" since 3:18 and 4:4. More importantly, he has not referred to idol worship as a problem. The worship of idols was a common problem both for Israel and for the early church, and the new covenant was to cleanse the people from idolatry (Ezek 36:25). It is unlikely that the author would introduce a new difficulty in the last line of the epistle. On the other hand, the reference to the true God in vs. 20 suggests the contrast that any false god or false view of God is idolatry—hence Grayston's description of this verse as "a finally wounding blow" against the elder's opponents (Grayston, p. 148). Theirs is not a higher or more enlightened theology; it is simply idolatry. The last line, understood in this way, summarizes the main concern of the epistle: the elder has written to those faithful and dear to him to protect them and to warn them to avoid the dangers posed by those who have left the community in order to propagate a deviant theology, which the elder regards as no more than false worship—and no better than idolatry.

Certainty and confidence are rare commodities in an age of skepticism, relativism, and pluralism. Sermons on "The Certainties of Faith" or "Of This We Can Be Sure" will receive a receptive hearing. These certainties protect those who believe in the name of the Son of God: they have eternal life (5:13); God hears and answers prayer (5:14–15); and prayer for one another can be life-giving (5:16–17). Finally, they can have confidence in God: the one born of God protects them (5:18); they belong to God (5:19); and the Son has given them saving knowledge of the one true God (5:20). Anything less than or contrary to that knowledge is, therefore, merely idolatry.

2 JOHN

A Warning to Guard the Truth

This brief epistle is closely related to 1 John. It may even owe its place in the NT to that association and the common assumption that it was written by the apostle John. All three epistles seem to have come from the leader of the Johannine community at the time of the departure of the group referred to in 1 John 2:19. The writer was sufficiently well known to identify himself simply as "the elder," but he did not have enough authority to give orders to the Johannine churches on the basis of his position or personal influence. Instead, he advises, requests, and appeals to the tradition of the church.

2 John was probably written shortly after the longer epistle. The sequence of the epistles could be reversed, as Houlden suggests, but the similarities between them are more easily explained as echoes than as expansions. 2 John contains phrases the author had only recently used in 1 John. While 1 John was a communication to the central Johannine community, 2 John is a true letter, written in contemporary Hellenistic letter form, to a sister church in a nearby town. The members of that church are warned about the teachings of those who had gone out from the Johannine community. They have departed from the received teachings. They are deceivers and antichrists, so do not even greet them when they come. The elder hopes to visit the sister church soon and will tell them more about the situation then.

Greeting: In Truth and Love (1–3)

The salutation follows the traditional letter form: A to B, greetings. In 2 John, however, the sender is identified by title rather than by name, the recipient is identified by a metaphorical reference ("an elect sister and her children"), and the greeting is delayed until after an elaborate description of the elder's relationship to the recipients in vss. 1b–2. The elder or presbyter was probably a member of the community who could claim the authority of its tradition by virtue of his association with those who had preceded him, perhaps even direct association with the Beloved Disciple. That he was the acknowledged leader of the Johannine community can be surmised from his use of the title "*the* elder." He may have been one of the last disciples of the Apostles, the church's link with the first generation. His position allowed him to give direction not only to the central Johannine community but to Johannine churches in other towns also, hence his ability to write both 2 and 3 John.

Although commentators have occasionally suggested that the *elect lady* was an individual Christian woman, perhaps named either "lady Electa" or "noble Kyria," it is now generally agreed that this title must refer to a sister church in the vicinity of the Johannine community. Her *children*, then, are fellow Johannine Christians who were in danger from the same group which had so disturbed the elder's community. In 1 John the elder addresses his readers as "my little children" (2:1); here the children belong to the "elect lady" (vss. 1, 4, 13).

The elder loves the elect lady's children *in truth*, because as fellow Johannine Christians who share the same tradition and the same beliefs, they too are "children of God." The phrase "in truth" may be adverbial, meaning no more than "truly," but both the significance of truth in the idiom of the Johannine writings and the repetition of the term five times in the first four verses of this letter suggest that it carries its full theological significance. As Johannine Christians, they have received grace and truth from Jesus Christ (John 1:14, 17), they do the truth (John 3:21), and they know the truth (John 8:32; 1 John 2:21) because they have the Spirit of Truth (John 14:17; 15:26; 16:13; 1 John 4:4, 6). *Truth* defines their origin, their relationship to God, and their way of life. It is the only sphere in which love is really possible, for perfect love (see 1 John 4:7–21) cannot be based on falsehood and deceit. The elder's love demands that he write; it also lays the highest claim to the right to be heard.

The elder is not alone in his love for this church, however. All of the Johannine Christians who have remained faithful to the truth are bound together by the new command to love one another (John 13:34–35; 1 John 2:7–11). Despite the disruption of the community, that command is being fulfilled. "Coming to know the truth" is tantamount to conversion and salvation in Johannine terms. It would mean believing in Jesus, grasping the revelation that has come through him, entering the community, and keeping the commandments.

Not only do Christians love in truth and know the truth; truth abides in them and will be with them forever. Verse 2, therefore, provides the theological basis for the love and knowledge professed in vs. 1. Elsewhere the Johannine writers speak of the Spirit of Truth abiding in the believers. The added assurance that they will possess the truth forever echoes John 14:16–17. It may have three implications: (1) they have eternal life; (2) although the Beloved Disciple has died, the truth will be with them forever; and (3) they cannot be torn from the truth by the dangers about which the elder will warn them. A general assurance such as the first alternative is most likely. The second is better suited to the context of the Gospel of John, and the third could not be emphasized without undermining the force of the following verses.

Verse 3 does not express a wish or prayer, as do greetings in other NT letters. It is a further assurance of God's blessings to all who belong to the truth: they have grace, mercy, and peace. The combination is unusual but occurs also in 1 Tim 1:2 and 2 Tim 1:2. *Mercy* does not occur anywhere else in the Johannine writings, and *grace* appears only in John's prologue. *Peace* is part of Jesus' legacy to his own, which is promised in the farewell discourse and fulfilled by the resurrection (John 14:27; 16:33; 20:19, 21, 26). The consistent sequence of these three aspects of Christian experience in the three verses in which they appear signals that they are probably a Christian formula in use in Asia Minor at the end of the first century. Grace is experienced in mercy and results in peace (SHALOM). God's grace is also experienced as he is known as Father, and is mediated by Jesus Christ. The designation "the Son of the Father" occurs only here in the NT but is thoroughly Johannine. The prepositional phrase at the end of vs. 3, "in truth and love," returns to the leitmotif of the greeting, and may be understood as meaning that it is in truth and love (key Johannine concepts) that grace, mercy, and peace (common early Christian, possibly Pauline, concepts) are experienced.

In the greeting, therefore, the elder establishes the basis for his communication to the church: his love for them in truth. In the process the greeting provides us with a profound reflection on the basis for fellowship between Christians and between churches. Is there any better statement of why or how we are to speak to one another? A sermon title for these verses might be "What Truth and Love Require," "The Basis of Christian Fellowship," or more provocatively "Baptists, Catholics, and Other Brand X Christians." Christian fellowship is circumscribed by truth and love, and the common experience of God's grace. If one enters by any other door, he is a robber and a thief (John 10).

Request: Love Those Who Walk in Truth (4–6)

Probably written on a single sheet of papyrus, 2 John follows the form and conventions of a Hellenistic letter as closely as any other in the NT. Following the greeting a thanksgiving was customary. A petition could open the body of a letter. The statement "I rejoiced greatly" often preceded the petition (see 3 John 3). 2 John follows this convention in detail. The cause for rejoicing is not the receipt of a letter from the other church but finding that its members are "walking in truth." Commentators have debated the nuances of vs. 4. Had the elder visited the other church recently? Had he received a visit from some of its members or from other Johannine Christians who knew the situation there? What is the force of the reference to "*some* of your children"? Does it mean there were others who were not faithful? The source of the elder's knowledge cannot be determined, yet what happens to his brothers and sisters there makes a difference to him. Since the thanksgiving and petition sections of a letter normally involved a commendation, it is unlikely that the reference to "some" intends any implication regarding others. The elder commends the church because so far as he knows they are "walking in the truth." This expression (see 3 John 3, 4) approximates the more common idiom of walking *in the light* (John 12:35; 1 John 1:7). It signifies the way of life which characterizes those who know the truth (vs. 1), have the truth abiding in them (vs. 2), and have found grace, mercy, and peace in truth (vs. 3). Such people can love in truth, and it is to this that the elder calls his fellow believers.

There is no command to "walk in truth" in the Gospel of John, so the elder must be referring either to the new command (as in the next verse) or, less likely, to the command to walk in the light (John 12:35–36). This command they have received from the Father. In the Gospel, Jesus refers to commands he has received from the Father (John 10:18; 14:31; 15:10). 1 John is unclear about whether "his" commands were received from Jesus or the Father (see 2:3–4; 3:22–24; 4:21; 5:2–3), but the difference is not significant since according to the Gospel, Jesus says only what he hears from the Father (John 5:19; 17:8). The two commands of the gospel (love, John 13:34; believe, John 14:1) are joined in 1 John 3:23. Similarly, following this reference to walking in truth, the elder writes about the requirements of brotherly love (vss. 5–6) and proper confession (vs. 7). Walking in truth, therefore, probably summarizes both the ethical and the doctrinal aspects of discipleship for Johannine Christians.

The petition follows immediately after the commendation: "And now I ask you ..." (vs. 5), but the elder is not asking as though he were writing some new requirement for them—he will later warn them about those who come making new demands on the church (vss. 9–10). Instead he is calling them back to a command which they have had "from the beginning" (1 John 2:7–8, 24). The "new commandment" has become an old one. They have heard it since they first heard the gospel. Indeed, it goes back to Jesus himself. His request is that "we" may love one another. By using the first-person plural, the elder includes himself and his community among those who have received the command, thereby softening it and implying that he stands with his readers. Perhaps the dissension within his own community has made him all the more aware of the need for unity among all Johannine Christians. He does not seem to be pleading that a ruptured relationship between the two churches be restored. On the contrary, he writes as one whose admonitions will be heeded, and he writes to shore up their relationship and prevent the kind of trouble the defecting group has caused within his own community.

Verse 6 clearly places emphasis on keeping the command to love, but its confusing repetition of tautologous statements makes confident exposition impossible. The first clause, "and this is love," points ahead and is explained by "that we walk in his commandments." This explanation amounts to little more than saying that love means keeping the commandment to love. Throughout these verses the elder appears to be speaking of love for one another rather than love for God. If the beginning of vs. 6 brings a change from love for one another to love for God, the elder would have needed to distinguish the movement of his thought more clearly. The commandment, "as you heard from the beginning" (see 1 John 2:24), is that you obey the command to love (see 1 John 5:3).

The Johannine community took the command to love one another as the center—and almost exclusive content—of its community ethic. The meaning of that command receives extensive explanation in 1 John 3:11–18 and 4:7–21. In Johannine dualism any who did not belong to the community of the truth belonged to the world, and there was no command to love them. As a result, the limits of community, which determined who is included in "one another," were crucial. Concern for truth led them to restrict the inclusiveness of their love, however. How can truth and love be the foci of the Christian community without restricting either truth or love too narrowly? Had the Johannine community missed some essential element of truth?

Warning: Do Not Receive Those Who Spread Deception (7–11)

The exhortation to unity within the Christian fellowship is followed by a warning against those who are alienated from it and will seek to destroy its faith. The first word of vs. 7, *for*, links the imperative to love one another to the danger posed by those who do not share their confession of Jesus Christ.

Verses 7 and 8 state a general warning against such deceivers. Verses 9–11 tell the church specifically how it may expect to encounter this threat and how it is to respond.

The elect lady is warned, "Many deceivers have gone out into the world." Every word of this warning rings with echoes from the Johannine materials. *Many* of Jesus' disciples left him at the collapse of his Galilean ministry (John 6:60, 66), many antichrists have come (1 John 2:18), and many false prophets have gone out into the world (1 John 4:1). *Deceivers* threaten the community because the deceivers deny that they have any sin (1 John 1:8; 2:26; 3:7). Like Judas Iscariot, these deceivers *have gone out* from the Christian fellowship (John 13:30; 1 John 2:19; 4:1). In Johannine dualism there is only the community of believers and the world opposed to Christ; one must belong to one or the other. To go out from the community, therefore, is to go out *into the world*, to become part of it (1 John 4:1; see 2:15–17).

These deceivers do not confess that Jesus Christ is coming, or has come, in flesh. Some interpreters take the first and more literal sense, contending that the error is denial of the return or parousia of the Lord. The similarity between vs. 7 and 1 John 4:2, however, has led most to interpret 2 John in the light of the more detailed description of the false teaching in 1 John. Accordingly, the problem is not denial of the parousia (as in 2 Peter 3:3–4) but denial of the incarnation (or at least denial of the significance of Jesus' ministry in the flesh). Those who do not confess Jesus in this way have no fellowship with God (1 John 2:22–23). They are deceivers and antichrists (see 1 John 2:18). They show that it is the last hour, and they are possessed by the Spirit of Deceit (1 John 4:6).

The warning, therefore, seems to concern those who had just recently gone out from the Johannine community. Believing in Jesus, the elder claims, means offering the proper confession, affirming not just that Jesus was the Christ (John 20:31) but that he came in flesh, with the attendant recognition of the significance of his ministry and death. The danger is not rejection but corruption of correct belief, and the danger had arisen within the community. The false prophets had separated from the community—they belong to the world—but still threaten the community.

Verse 8 heightens the urgency of the situation: "Watch out!" The danger was that the faithful might lose what they had worked for and fail to receive their reward, but what, specifically, does the elder have in mind? Is he referring to their faith or their eternal life, their heavenly rewards, or the converts they have brought to faith? Most commentators have chosen the first as the most likely; the believers have worked for their faith (John 6:27, 29) and eternal life is their reward (John 20:31; 1 John 2:25). There is no basis in the Gospel or Epistles for thinking that the elder is referring to some further heavenly reward. It is possible, however, that he has their missionary work in mind, the growth of the church. Jesus lost none of those who were given to him, except Judas (John 6:39; 17:12; 18:9). The faithful have been doing God's work (John 6:27–29). Now, however, as a result of the destructive work of the deceivers, they may lose their reward. The only other occurrence of *reward* in the Gospel and Epistles is in John 4:36 (see Rev 11:18; 22:12), where in connection with the mission to the Samaritans Jesus says that the missionary will have a reward and gather fruit for eternal life. The deceivers threaten all those the community has brought to faith in Jesus Christ. The church deserves its *full* reward (see Ruth 2:12), the fullness of life that comes from Jesus (John 1:14, 16), and eternal life for all who share its faith. Only then can their joy be complete (1 John 1:4).

Verses 9–11 relate the apocalyptic warning of the preceding verses regarding the work of the antichrist to the danger the church may face from traveling teachers or missionaries. Verse 9 can be read as a very repressive condemnation of any new ideas or theological developments. As C. H. Dodd remarked, "The writer has incautiously expressed himself in terms which might seem to stigmatize any kind of 'advance' as disloyalty to the faith, and so to condemn Christian theology to lasting sterility" (*The Johannine Epistles*, p. 150). But the elder does not intend such a general condemnation. After all, the bold theological developments of the Gospel of John mark the Johannine tradition and are authorized as the work of the Paraclete. Here the elder charges that some have moved so far in their thinking that they no longer abide in Christ's teaching. Although *abiding* is a common Johannine concept, this is the only place where it is used in connection

with teaching. Elsewhere the believer is urged to abide in
Christ or in God, but abiding in the teaching of Christ is not
materially different from abiding in what they heard from
the beginning (1 John 2:24, see 2:27) or having his word abiding in them (1 John 2:14). This teaching of Christ, then, is
primarily the tradition received from the Beloved Disciple
and transmitted by the Johannine school, not a doctrine
about Christ. The deceivers neither practice the command to
love nor hold to the confession of Jesus Christ come in flesh
(vs. 7). Although this verse does not represent a sharp departure from the elder's exhortations elsewhere in the Epistles,
one may nevertheless detect that the church is taking a further step toward defining orthodoxy in terms of the approved
teachings of the church, which are protected by tradition.
Those who do not abide in these teachings do not "have God"
(see 1 John 2:23). On the other hand, those who abide in this
teaching also "have" or abide in both the Father and the Son
(1 John 2:24).

Based on this distinction, the elder advises the sister
church that if travelers come to them who do not convey this
teaching, they should not receive them into the house or even
greet them. The travelers in question here would be religious
teachers, probably purporting to be fellow Johannine Christians. The elder recognizes that those who have gone out
from his community (1 John 2:19) may now attempt to gain
adherents and spread their teaching in the Johannine
churches in neighboring towns. We do not know whether 2
John was sent to the only other sister church. Since 3 John
appears to have a separate situation in view, it may be that
there were several sister churches. If so, copies of 2 John may
have been sent to several different churches. The *house*
would be a house church. Early Christian mission work de-
pended heavily on the practice of hospitality (Mark 9:37;
Rom 12:13; 1 Peter 4:9), and other early Christian writings
show that the church developed rules for dealing with the
problems which could be created by itinerant preachers and
teachers (Mark 6:7–11; 2 Cor 11:4; *Didache* 11:1–2). Paul
warned the Philippians to beware of "evil-workers," apparently referring to itinerants preaching a Judaizing gospel
(Phil 3:2).

Here the elder instructs the church to defend itself from

false teaching by not even extending a greeting to those who propagate a different teaching (vs. 11). By extending a greeting, he warns, one has entered into fellowship with the deceiver and participates in his evil works. One has "aided and abetted" the enemy and assisted in their evil works by making it possible for them to spread their false teaching among the faithful. The devil is "the evil one" (1 John 2:13–14). The antichrists who have gone out into the world are children of the devil, and like Cain their works are evil (see 1 John 2:18; 3:10, 12; 5:19). The rigid theological dualism of the Johannine community, therefore, contributed to its division. Members of house churches linked to the Johannine community were warned not even to speak to those who had pulled away from or been driven out of the elder's community.

3 John, however, shows that other church leaders, such as Diotrephes, could refuse to receive those who were sent by the elder. C. H. Dodd, noting the ineffectiveness of such a procedure, warns that this is obviously an extreme measure and emergency regulations make bad laws for less troubled periods:

> Does truth prevail the more if we are not on speaking terms with those whose view of the truth differs from ours—however disastrous their error may be? . . . The problem is to find a way of living with those whose convictions differ from our own upon the most fundamental matters, without either breaking charity or being disloyal to the truth (*The Johannine Epistles*, p. 152).

Closing: The Fulfillment of Joy (12–13)

It was common for letters to close with some review of why the letter was written, the promise of a visit, and a farewell or statement of greetings. Just as the Gospel of John closes with the statement that Jesus did many other signs (John 20:30; 21:25; see 3 John 13), so the elder declares that he has many other things to say to them. He does not want to put these in writing, however. *Why*, one might ask. Does he not want to go further into detail about the dissension in the community? Does he not wish to identify anyone by name in writing? Or is the statement simply a perfunctory way of drawing the letter to a close as the writer nears the end of a sheet of papyrus?

Some (e.g., Houlden) have taken this statement, with the accompanying hope of a visit, as a basis for suggesting that the visit never materialized and 1 John was subsequently written to convey the "many other things" the elder wanted to say to them. On the other hand, the differences in the situations portrayed in the letters and in the elder's manner of addressing the recipients make it difficult to consider that the two letters were written to the same audience, whatever their sequence. The specific problem addressed in 2 John, itinerant teachers who will come bearing a false teaching, is not addressed at all in 1 John. According to the longer letter, these false prophets have *gone out* from the community.

The purpose of a visit would be "that our joy may be fulfilled" (vs. 12). Some manuscripts read "your joy," but "our" is consistent with 1 John 1:4. It is characteristic of the Johannine Gospel and Epistles to use *joy* with *fulfilled*, often declaring the hope that their joy may be fulfilled (John 3:29; 15:11; 16:24; 17:13; 1 John 1:4). Such statements imply that the believers already have an eschatological joy, but acknowledge that it is not yet complete (see John 16:20–22).

The closing formula (vs. 13), which conveys greetings from "the children of your elect sister," resumes the metaphor of the letter's address: "to the elect lady and her children" (vs. 1). Greetings are offered at the conclusion of most of Paul's letters, and close parallels to 2 John 13 may also be found in 1 Peter 5:13, Heb 13:24, and 3 John 15. *Elect* is not a common term in the Johannine writings, since it occurs only in 2 John 1 and 13 (and in some texts of John 1:34). Running through the Gospel, however, are affirmations of God's initiative in calling, giving, and drawing his own (see John 6:37, 44; 10:3, 27; 17:9, 12). Understandably, therefore, the elder speaks of all the Johannine Christians who remain faithful as "the elect." Following his metaphorical language, the churches are elect sisters, and the individual believers are their children. They belong to the family of the "children of God" (John 1:12). God has chosen the church to be his family, "the family of God."

Truth and love are the cardinal virtues of this family of faith. Both its beliefs and its fellowship must reflect the integrity of truth. If God is the ultimate reality and truth is that which conforms to reality, then the community of faith can only be true to its calling by maintaining unity both with God's Spirit and with fellow believers. Although the twin virtues of the Johannine Epistles have proved to be as elusive for later Christians as they were for the first-century churches, no church can strive for less without compromising its loyalty to the family. The ideals of 2 John stand as an enduring challenge for the church, therefore, even if we would choose other practical measures than the ones it recommends as means for attaining those ideals.

The message of 2 John can be packaged in sermons labeled "Trouble in the Family," "Truth and Love in Conflict," or "A House Divided." (Did you see the news story about the man who took a saw and cut his house in half when he divorced his wife? See Mark 3:25.) These sermons can foster church unity in the context of a local congregation, denominations threatened by schism, or ecumenicity stymied by exaggerated denominationalism.

3 JOHN

An Appeal for Hospitality

Several superlatives distinguish 3 John: it is the shortest letter of the NT, the only book of the NT which does not mention Jesus or Christ, and the only Johannine writing to mention *the church* (vss. 6, 9, 10). 3 John is also one of the most enigmatic NT writings. Because of the similarities with 2 John, it is commonly assumed that 3 John was written by the same author, "the elder." 3 John is addressed to an individual, Gaius, whom the elder praises for his hospitality to itinerant Johannine Christians. The elder solicits Gaius's support against Diotrephes, who high-handedly rejected the elder's emissaries and refused to acknowledge the elder's authority. The elder also commends Demetrius to Gaius as one who is true. In conclusion, the elder promises a visit and extends a greeting from "the friends."

Beyond these essential facts, the situation assumed in 3 John is difficult to describe with any confidence. Questions abound. Who are each of the three individuals named in the letter—Gaius, Diotrephes, and Demetrius? What was their relationship to each other and to the elder? What positions, if any, did they hold in the church? Did Gaius belong to the same house church as Diotrephes? Was the problem simply one of organization and leadership or were there doctrinal differences between the elder and Diotrephes? Was Diotrephes related in any way to the false prophets and deceivers described in 1 and 2 John? Answers to these questions will be suggested below, but readers should recognize that

interpreters are divided on these issues. The letter allows for
various plausible interpretations.

Because it contains no profound theological discussion, 3
John might easily be neglected. There was wisdom in its inclusion in the canon, however. It provides a rewarding
glimpse into the difficulty of working out harmonious relations between Johannine house churches, or between the
Johannine community and satellite churches. The damage
which can be caused by rivalry among church leaders is evident in 3 John, as is an even more significant point: the importance of unity and cooperation in fulfilling the mission of the
church is so great that the church cannot allow either personal differences or demands for theological uniformity to
stand in the way of unity and cooperative mission efforts. Harmony, in fact, depends on diversity, not uniformity. Sermons
on 3 John should treat the epistle as a whole, describe the
historical situation, and offer harmony and cooperation as an-
tidotes to the jealousy and rivalry that often arise in church
life. The following titles suggest different ways in which one
might preach on 3 John: "When Good Intentions Become Destructive," "Diotrephes or Demetrius? Two Styles of Christian
Service," "No Greater Joy" (vs. 4), "Becoming Fellow Workers
in the Truth" (vs. 8), "The Consequences of Putting Yourself
First" (vs. 9), and "Peace in the Church" (vs. 15).

Greetings to a Beloved Brother (1–4)

The letter begins with the same opening as 2 John: "The
elder to x, whom I love in truth." The twin emphases on truth
and love are combined here, as they are in 2 John. The elder is
presumably known to Gaius, since he does not need to identify
himself by name. The recipient, "Gaius the beloved," should
probably not be identified with any of the other NT figures
with this name (Acts 19:29; 20:4; Rom 16:23; 1 Cor 1:14). As a
fellow Johannine Christian, charged with the command to love
one another, Gaius is "beloved." To love in truth means to love
within the experience and knowledge of God's love, revealed by
Jesus (see the comment on 2 John 1).

Verse 2 begins with the common Johannine address, "beloved," which also marks the beginning of two other
paragraphs in 3 John (vss. 5 and 11; see 1 John 2:7; 3:2,21;
4:1, 7, 11). A comment expressing the hope that the recipient

is in good health generally followed the salutation in Hellenistic letters, and 3 John follows this formula more closely
than any other letter in the NT. The wish for good health is
followed by the hope that Gaius is "having a good journey,"
and is matched at the end of the verse with the hope that his
psyche is also enjoying a "good journey." *Psyche* is used in
the Johannine writings for that life which one can lay down
(not one's eternal life; see John 10:11, 15, 17; 12:25; 13:37, 38;
15:13; 1 John 3:16).

Just as in 2 John 4, the elder expresses great joy at the
reports that his brother in Christ is walking in truth. "Brothers" are coming to the elder and testifying concerning Gaius.
The brothers are presumably fellow Johannine Christians, as
elsewhere in these epistles, who have been traveling among
the Johannine churches. On the basis of the problems with
traveling Christians discussed in 2 John and in the remainder of 3 John, it is clear that these brothers carried true
teachings, not those of the defectors. Whether they had been
sent out by the elder or merely worked in partnership with
him is not so clear. Presumably they had been well treated
by Gaius and had returned with the report that he was walking in truth because he practiced love for "the brothers."
Doctrine is not an issue; we may assume that Gaius held to a
correct Christology. The elder is not concerned with Christology in 3 John as he is in the other two epistles.

The elder's greatest joy comes from hearing that his children are walking in the truth. With this statement the elder
reveals that he has a pastor's heart. In the parallel statement
in 2 John 4 he refers to his fellow Johannine Christians as the
elect lady's children, but here as in 1 John they are *his* children. Even though there is no evidence of prior contact between the elder and Gaius, he includes Gaius among his own,
from whom he expects compliance. Referring to Gaius as one
of his children served to remind Gaius of the basis of their
fellowship and the basis for the requests that would follow.
With subtle tact, therefore, the elder insures that he will have
Gaius's continuing cooperation.

Praise for Gaius's Hospitality (5–8)

The petition section of the letter opens with further, more
specific praise for Gaius. He showed his faithfulness by what

he did for the brothers, especially since they were strangers to him. The picture conveyed is that Gaius had been receiving faithful Johannine Christians who traveled to his city, even though he was not closely tied in to the network of hospitality practiced within the Johannine churches. By means of this letter, the elder hoped to encourage Gaius to continue to show hospitality to the itinerants who carried the elder's teachings, even when they were opposed by Diotrephes. There is no evidence that Gaius was the head of a house church. He had simply distinguished himself by his willingness to provide hospitality for fellow Christians. In doing so he was showing his faithfulness.

The Johannine "missionaries" were so impressed by Gaius's generosity that they bore witness to his love before the church. Hospitality was a sign of love (vs. 6), which confirmed that Gaius lived in the truth (vs. 3). Since vs. 3 said that the brothers had *come* with a report regarding Gaius, we may assume that they had testified regarding Gaius before the elder's church.

The main purpose of the letter is delicately stated in the commendation in vs. 6. Gaius has done well and will continue to do well by receiving itinerant Johannine Christians, offering them hospitality and speeding them on their way. In doing so he was living in a way "worthy of God" (see Col 1:10; 1 Thess 2:12).

Gaius's actions have been "worthy of God" because the Johannine missionaries set out in the name of Jesus (see 1 John 2:12; 3:23; 5:13), and Jesus had come in his Father's name (see John 5:43; 10:25; 12:13). What Gaius was doing was worthy of God, because it was part of what the Father was giving the believers in Jesus' name (John 16:23). It may even be regarded as a part of the Father's keeping believers in Jesus' name (John 17:11). The Johannine itinerants did not receive anything from the pagans. Here *pagans* does not mean "Gentiles," since the three names which appear in 3 John are all gentile names: Gaius, Diotrephes, and Demetrius. The issue of divisions between Jewish and Gentile believers is not a problem here and has not been mentioned anywhere in the Johannine Epistles. Instead, *pagans* is close to "the world," which will not receive believers because they bear Jesus' name. The world does not know the one who sent Jesus, either (John 15:21). The practice of receiving nothing from unbelievers means that the Johannine itinerants were totally dependent on the generosity of fellow Christians, such as Gaius. Without their hospitality the church would be crippled, its fellowship would be destroyed, and its mission would be paralyzed.

Verse 8 draws an important conclusion. The believers ought to help such ones, the travelers, so that they might be fellow workers in the truth. The obligation grows out of their relationship to Jesus Christ (see John 13:14; 1 John 2:6; 3:16; 4:11). Hospitality is a specific example of walking as Jesus walked, loving one another, and washing one another's feet. Because the itinerants receive nothing from unbelievers, they ought all the more to be received by believers. Gaius is an example of one who "has the world's goods," because he is apparently a householder who is able to provide hospitality for others, but he did not "close his heart"—or his doors—when he saw a brother in need (1 John 3:17). The love of God abides in such as Gaius! Although he was not an itinerant, he was a "fellow worker in the truth." Paul often spoke of his *fellow workers* (see Rom 16:3; 1 Cor 3:9; Phil 2:25; 4:3). *Worker* was a title given to evangelists and itinerants (see Matt 9:37–38; 2 Cor 11:13; Phil 3:2), and the mission could be referred to as *the work* (Acts 14:26; 15:38). Gaius's hospitality was work (vs. 5), and by means of it he not only showed himself as one who walked in truth and love but also paradoxically became more of what he already was.

The importance of hospitality is further illustrated by the irony that at about the same time the elder wrote 3 John, he also wrote 2 John urging "the elect sister" not to extend hospitality to any who did not share their Christology. Such itinerants were deceivers and antichrists (2 John 7). By receiving false teachers they could destroy that for which they had *worked* (2 John 8). Presumably, by receiving deceivers they would become fellow workers of deceit, just as Gaius was a fellow worker of the truth. The elder's hope as he writes is that Gaius will continue to be a "fellow worker in truth," but he knows that Gaius will face opposition.

Criticism of Diotrephes' Defiance (9–10)

The reason why the elder appealed to Gaius for hospitality and support now emerges. He had already written to the church, but his initiatives were blocked by Diotrephes. Various theories have been advanced to explain the relationship between the elder and Diotrephes. Dodd suggested that Diotrephes either was "the first monarchical bishop" in the area or had "usurped quasi-episcopal functions." Käsemann reversed conventional interpretations by contending that Diotrephes was a representative of the orthodox church who had rejected the elder because of his gnostic heresies. Diotrephes' "office" is no clearer than that of the elder, who as we have seen does not invoke the authority of an office in any of these epistles. The restraint of 3 John, moreover, and the notable absence of the strident language of 1 and 2 John suggest that the differences between the elder and Diotrephes were not doctrinal. Diotrephes was not one of the antichrists, false prophets, or deceivers who had gone out from the community. He had asserted himself as the leader of the church, however, and had severed relations with the elder.

When the elder declares that he had written *something* to the church it is unlikely that he is referring to either 1 or 2 John. Those epistles dealt with the problem created by those who had left the church over doctrinal differences; here the elder's concern is hospitality and cooperation for fellow Johannine Christians traveling among the Johannine churches. The elder wrote to the church, but Diotrephes, "who loves to put himself first among them," would not receive "us" (vs. 9). The elder's comment suggests that Diotrephes did not hold an appointed or elected office but simply assumed authority within one of the Johannine churches. The elder had assumed that the church would be responsive, but Diotrephes blocked his efforts. Since the elder speaks of *them*, it may be that Gaius was not a member of the church controlled by Diotrephes, which would explain why the elder must tell Gaius what has taken place. If Gaius was a member of the same church as Diotrephes, the reports from the brothers (vss. 3, 6) led the elder to believe that Gaius might nevertheless continue to cooperate with the elder and those loyal to him. *Us* may be either the Johannine school (i.e., those who represented the tradition of the Beloved Disciple) or those who remained faithful to the elder following the schism of the community (see John 21:24; 1 John 1:1–4; 2:19; 3 John 12). The report that Diotrephes did

not receive them may mean either that he did not receive the
elder or those sent by him when they attempted to visit the
church, or that Diotrephes would not receive or acknowledge
the letter. In asserting his leadership Diotrephes rejected the
authority of the elder to speak to the church, and severed
communication with the elder. 3 John therefore represents at
least the second attempt the elder made to preserve some
sort of cordial relations and entrée with the church.

If the elder comes to the church, he will bring up what
Diotrephes is doing. The elder has apparently not decided
whether to make the trip or not (see vs. 14), but if he comes
he will deal with the problem he has had with Diotrephes. To
whom will he recall Diotrephes' "works"? Gaius? Diotrephes? the church? Gaius's church or Diotrephes'? Perhaps
the alternatives should not be pressed. The elder will deal
with the problem with the Christians in that area, just as the
brothers coming from Gaius have testified to the church
where the elder lives (vss. 3, 6).

The remainder of vs. 10 states four specific actions Diotrephes has taken: (1) babbling or prating against the elder
with evil words, (2) refusing to receive the brothers, (3) hin-
dering those who are willing to receive them, and (4) casting
such people out of the church. These actions show that Diotrephes does not merely want to "put himself first." He has
already done so and effectively controls the church. The
charge that Diotrephes chatters with *evil words* is the strong-
est charge the elder makes and the closest he comes to using
the dualistic language of 1 and 2 John (see 1 John 3:12; 2
John 11). Not being satisfied merely to create dissension
among the churches by his idle talk, Diotrephes apparently
severed his church from the network or fellowship of Johannine churches. By not receiving the itinerant *brothers*, Diotrephes used the same tactic the elder advised in 2 John. It
remains unclear whether Diotrephes was (1) aligned with the
deceivers who held to a false Christology, (2) in agreement
with the elder theologically but unable to distinguish the
false teachers from the brothers, or (3) unconcerned about
the schism that had plagued the elder's community and
merely asserting his and the church's independence from the
(central?) Johannine community. The first alternative can
probably be excluded because the elder does not deal with

Christology or use the dualistic language as he did in 1 and 2 John. If the second alternative is taken, Diotrephes refused to accept all itinerants in an effort to protect the church from false teachings, or he may have refused to receive brothers, thinking they were "deceivers" (2 John 7) claiming to be fellow Johannine Christians. How did those who had gone out from the Johannine community present themselves when they visited and sought hospitality from a sister church? The third alternative has little to commend it but cannot be excluded. There is no reason to impugn Diotrephes' motives unnecessarily.

Diotrephes apparently regarded the issue as a very serious matter, however. Not only did he refuse to receive the brothers, he stopped others from doing so and excluded from the church those who extended hospitality to the traveling brothers. How he may have hindered others from receiving the travelers is not clear, but apparently with "evil words" and the threat to expel them from the church. Again, Diotrephes may have been able to *cast out* such members simply by his own decree, or he may have led the church to do so. However it was done, the elder implies that exclusion was not merely a threat but had actually occurred. By casting members out of the fellowship, Diotrephes disrupted the fellowship (*koinonia*), violated the promise of Jesus in John 6:37 ("him who comes to me I will not cast out"), and practiced instead the policy of the synagogue which had excluded those who confessed Jesus as Messiah (John 9:22, 34–35). This "all or nothing" approach to church discipline would be practiced with destructive results in the late nineteenth and early twentieth centuries.

From these verses we can see that 3 John reflects the growing pains of a community of churches attempting to work out cooperative relations and yet defend themselves against unacceptable teachings. This problem persists both within denominations and between Christian denominations. 3 John may continue to serve, therefore, as both a call for cooperative efforts and a reminder of the dissension which so often strikes churches when harsh measures are taken to exclude certain beliefs, when communication between individuals and churches is broken, or when church leaders allow personal ambitions to influence their actions.

Praise for Demetrius' Truthfulness (11–12)

The last point of the letter, before the formalities of the closing verses, is to commend Demetrius to Gaius. Verse 11 opens with a repetition of the address *beloved*, which marked the beginning of earlier paragraphs in vss. 2 and 5. The verse forms a transition back to the appeal for hospitality, which was the subject of vss. 5 to 8. The command to *imitate* was common in some Hellenistic ethical materials and in Paul's letters, but does not occur elsewhere in the Johannine writings. The contrast here is also distinctive: "not the bad but the good." *The bad* occurs in John 18:23, 30 in connection with charges against Jesus, and *the good* occurs only three times in John, and nowhere else in the Epistles of John. In this context, the maxim seems to be used to point to Diotrephes as one who does bad and Demetrius as an example of one who does good. 1 John speaks of those who do the truth (1:10) and justice (2:29; 3:10), and who show love for their brothers (4:7); they are *from God*. Those who belong to God shall see him (1 John 3:2); but one who does not love his brother, whom he has seen, cannot love God, whom he has not seen (1 John 4:21). The end of vs. 11 restates 1 John 3:6: one who sins has not seen God. In this instance receiving the itinerant brothers is *doing good* and refusing to receive them, i.e., *doing bad*, shows that one has not seen God. With this implicit charge against Diotrephes the elder comes close to excluding him from the church!

Demetrius is introduced rather abruptly in vs. 12, and so little is said about him that we are left with more questions than answers. All we are told is that (1) everyone testifies for him, (2) the truth itself testifies for him, and (3) *we* testify for him. This threefold testimony forms a strong statement of commendation for Demitrius. Was Demetrius a member of Diotrephes' church who had been excluded from the church for defying Diotrephes by receiving the itinerant brothers? If so, the contrast suggested in vs. 11 between those who do good and those who do bad is balanced. On the other hand, it is more likely that Demetrius is one of the traveling brothers who will need hospitality. If so, he has not stayed with Gaius before and is still unknown to him. He may even be the bearer of the letter, and may have been one of those rejected by Diotrephes.

Whatever the precise background may be, the elder ends the body of the letter with this commendation for Demetrius. The *all* who bear witness to him must be actually all the faithful Johannine Christians who know him. His character and work have such integrity and soundness that truth itself testifies for him. As elsewhere in the Epistles, *truth* stands for all that belongs to God, is revealed by Jesus, and characterizes the life of the faithful believers who practice love for one another. *We* may be an editorial "we," meaning the elder himself, but in view of the statement at the end of vs. 12 it is more likely a reference to the Johannine school. This would presumably be a narrower group than the *all* referred to earlier. Those at the core of the community, who derived their tradition and authority from their association with the Beloved Disciple, also endorsed Demetrius (see the *we* in John 21:24; 1 John 1:1–4).

The final clause of vs. 12 echoes the "imprimatur," used by the Johannine community to certify that truth had been declared:

> John 19:35—He who saw it has borne witness—his testimony is true, and he knows that he tells the truth— that you also may believe.

> John 21:24—This is the disciple who is bearing witness to these things, and who has written these things; and we know that his testimony is true. (RSV)

Now Gaius is reminded that he should acknowledge the authority of the elder. Gaius should receive Demetrius as a brother.

Demetrius, who is just a shadow figure in the NT, is nevertheless a worthy ideal for all Christians. What sort of person could deserve such high praise? Of whom would we say "truth itself bears them witness"? The tragedy is that it was apparently the division in the church and the harsh measures taken by Diotrephes which required that the elder add this note of recommendation. Still, although there were deceivers and others who did wrong, there were some like Gaius and Demetrius whose grasp of truth was firm and who would not be deterred from showing love in hospitality so that the work of the church could continue.

Peace for "the Friends" (13–15)

The closing verses of 3 John closely parallel the ending of 2 John. Verses 13–14 claim that the elder had many other things to say but preferred not to put them on paper, hoping soon to be able to speak face to face. Verse 15 extends greetings and uses the distinctive term *friends*. Reading the closing verses of each letter in English one sees their similarities but may miss the fact that in expression they differ in virtually every phrase.

The elder has *many things* to write to Gaius. On the basis of what we know from 1 and 2 John, the reader may be tempted to speculate that Gaius does not know the full picture of the division in the Johannine community and the elder does not wish to go into these matters in a personal letter. The promise of *many things* has a well-established currency in the Johannine writings, however. According to the Gospel, Jesus had many things to say to the Jews (John 8:26) and many things yet to say to the disciples (John 16:12). Many other things could have been written (John 21:25) because he did many works and signs (John 10:32; 11:47). The closing verses of 3 John begin with the same assertion; the letter does not say all that the elder wants to say. He did not need to write these things because he hoped to come soon. This statement, that he hopes to come soon, is more affirmative than either vs. 10, "if I come," or the parallel statement at the end of 2 John.

The pronouncement of peace follows longstanding Jewish and early Christian custom, but in 3 John it also echoes the Gospel's assurance that Jesus would leave *his* peace with the disciples (see John 14:27; 16:33; 20:19, 21, 26). Similarly, the greetings from *the friends* (*philoi*) emphasized the *koinonia* of the Johannine Christians with one another. *Friends* here probably conveys more than the normal sense of the word. The Gospel of John refers to John the Baptist as a friend of the bridegroom (John 3:29); Lazarus, to whom Jesus gives life, is a friend (11:11); and Jesus lays down his life for his friends (15:13–15). *Friends*, therefore, seems to be similar in meaning to *brothers* (vss. 3, 5, 10), *children* (2 John 1, 13), or *beloved* (vss. 1, 2, 5, 11). The "friends" are beloved brothers and sisters, faithful members of the Johannine churches who are still loyal to the elder. The term expressed their relationship to one another and to their Lord. The "friends" are to be greeted *by name*, just as the good shepherd called his sheep by name (John 10:3). By analogy, like the sheep who know the shepherd's voice, those who remain loyal to the elder should receive his greetings and honor his request for hospitality for their brothers.

3 John is the counterpart to 2 John. 2 John warns a sister church to guard the truth, especially their belief in Jesus who came in flesh. The warning was needed because traveling deceivers would come to the church spreading false teachings. 3 John appeals for support and hospitality for faithful brothers traveling to spread the gospel. The appeal was necessary because Diotrephes was refusing hospitality to faithful brothers. Deceivers and friends were apparently using the same methods both for propagating their beliefs and for excluding those with whom they disagreed. What a tangled web the church can weave.

The difference between deceivers and brothers, according to all three epistles, is that the faithful believers hold to the truth that has been conveyed to them, they obey Jesus' commands, and they practice love for one another. By doing so they show that they are the children of God.

Bibliography

It is time to pass the baton once more. The commentaries on the Johannine Epistles are surprisingly ample and varied. Raymond E. Brown, *The Epistles of John*, Anchor Bible, vol. 30 (Garden City, N.Y.: Doubleday, 1982), has elevated the art of commentary writing to a new standard. His commentary provides detailed discussion of all the relevant textual, grammatical, historical, and theological problems while fairly and succinctly summarizing positions taken by previous commentators. It is an encyclopedia of Johannine theology. In contrast to Brown's focus on the schism of the community, C. H. Dodd interpreted the Epistles within the broader context of Greco-Roman culture and religious thought: *The Johannine Epistles*, Moffatt Commentaries (London: Hodder and Stoughton, 1946).

Other recent commentaries include: F. F. Bruce, *The Epistles of John* (Grand Rapids: Wm. B. Eerdmans, 1970); Rudolf Bultmann, *The Johannine Epistles*, Hermeneia (Philadelphia: Fortress Press, 1973); Kenneth Grayston, *The Johannine Epistles*, New Century Bible (Grand Rapids: Wm. B. Eerdmans, 1984); J. L. Houlden, *The Johannine Epistles*, Harper's New Testament Commentaries (New York: Harper & Row, 1973); I. Howard Marshall, *The Epistles of John*, New International Commentary (Grand Rapids: Wm. B. Eerdmans, 1978); Pheme Perkins, *The Johannine Epistles*, New Testament Message (Wilmington, Del.: Michael Glazier, 1979); and Stephen S. Smalley, *1, 2, 3 John*, Word Biblical Commentary (Waco, Tx: Word Books, 1984).

Two recent dissertations make significant contributions: John Bogart, *Orthodox and Heretical Perfectionism*, SBL Dissertation Series, 33 (Missoula: Scholars Press, 1977); Edward Malatesta, *Interiority and Covenant*, Analecta Biblica, 69 (Rome: Biblical Institute Press, 1978).

The *Review and Expositor*, 67 (Fall 1970), was devoted to the Johannine Epistles and contains a helpful article on preaching from these epistles.